The Science of Management

Fighting Fads and Fallacies with Evidence-Based Practice

Dr Simon Moss and Dr Ronald Francis

Monash University

AUSTRALIAN ACADEMIC PRESS
Brisbane

First published in 2007 by
Australian Academic Press
32 Jeays Street
Bowen Hills QLD 4006
Australia
www.australianacademicpress.com.au

National Library of Australia
Cataloguing-in-Publication data:

Moss, Simon.
    The science of management: fighting fads and fallacies
    with evidence-based practice

    1st ed.
    Bibliography.
    ISBN 9781875378784 (pbk.).

    1. Personnel management - Decision making. 2. Management -
    Research. I. Francis, Ronald. II. Title.

    658.30072

Cover and text design by Maria Biaggini of Australian Academic Press, Brisbane.

Contents

Table of Contents   iii

Contents
(continued)

What Is This Book About?

To enhance the performance of their employees and their company, managers and supervisors need to reach an extraordinary number of decisions every day. Usually, these decisions seem straightforward and based on information from many sources — training programs, management literature, discussions with peers as well as experience and instinct.

A city cafe manager might feel certain that using modern jazz for his background music will help business. A general manager might decide to introduce an open plan office to promote cooperation amongst employees. Or a chief executive officer might decide to form specific workgroups of employees who exhibit similar skills, values and interests.

But are the assumptions and beliefs behind these decisions actually correct?

Research indicates that classical music has been demonstrated to increase sales in restaurants more than other styles of music, that open plan offices may actually impair cooperation amongst colleagues up to six months after they are introduced, and that workgroups in which the skills, values and interests of employees are diverse, not uniform, can be more innovative, effective and even cohesive.

However, today's managers may be too busy to uncover this research themselves or unaware of how to find management information that is evidence-based rather than derived from the latest management fad, personal opinion, anecdotal observation, pseudo-research, or even just a dogged preference for the status quo.

To address these problems, the authors decided to collate, from an analysis of almost 16,000 scientific articles, useful findings for managers, uncovering along the way over 800 surprising discoveries that contradict common management practices and conflict with most individuals' intuition. This book presents some of these key discoveries organised around the core management responsibilities of:

- workplace objectives
- team performance
- individual performance
- addressing undesirable behaviour
- promoting employee wellbeing
- recruitment and selection

Managers, supervisors, and consultants who would like to question conventional practices could read this book from cover to cover or could proceed to the sections that discuss issues they currently need to address. Employees could read this book, either to improve their own work life or to influence the behavior of managers. Psychology, human resource and management students could also read this publication to develop expertise and knowledge that most of their peers will not acquire.

Testing Your Insight

As you open this book — perhaps earnest, dubious or even downright sceptical — you may suddenly experience a sense of disappointment, irritation or disdain. Another futile publication on management, one more volume emphasising skills or expertise that cannot be extracted from a book and instead intended to challenge behaviours, practices and policies you have successfully followed for many years.

Yet this book is not merely another management text. Sure, it claims to be unique, practical and invaluable like every other management publication; but unlike many other publications, this book realises these claims, by offering suggestions that are surprising and validated rather than obvious or unproven.

So before you form too quick a judgment, try completing the questionnaire on page 4 now. After completing the questionnaire, you may have regarded the questions as ambiguous. Perhaps you decided, or at least hoped, that none of these statements are necessarily true or false. If so, your assumptions are incorrect. Each of these statements has been rigorously tested using the latest scientific paradigms, tools and methodologies. All of these statements are false.

This exercise reveals that many of the beliefs, opinions and assumptions that underlie our decisions, guide our behaviours or motivate our initiatives may be untenable. We might assume that managers should reward employees who refrain from discrimination and harassment. We might encourage employees to follow all rules and regulations, rigidly and precisely, or closely monitor employees who are not performing effectively — yet all of these assumptions and beliefs are erroneous (see Monin & Miller, 2001; Witowski & Streinsmeier-Pelster, 1998). Indeed, many of our behaviours and decisions may unwittingly damage rather than advance the performance of employees and workgroups.

A few managers become defensive when informed that some of their knowledge, beliefs and opinions — assumptions that drive all of their behaviours — are so misguided. They deny their beliefs are flawed or that these misconceptions are consequential. They feel their intuition is sound and regard their instincts as accurate. However, these managers may be unaware of the biases and distortions that inflate their perceptions of themselves. For instance, research findings show that managers are less likely to remember the occasions in which their predictions were not confirmed or their assumptions were contradicted. As a consequence of this bias, as well as countless other fallacies, the majority of managers overestimate how often their intuition is correct.

Nevertheless, we do not need to become defensive. These flaws and misconceptions provide an opportunity to advance

	True	False
When individuals lie to another person they are less likely to pause during sentences, especially if the other person does not seem at all suspicious	❏	❏
When individuals feel compelled to condemn some activity, such as a risky act, they are less likely to undertake that activity in the future	❏	❏
Relative to other commercials, advertisements that appear during TV programs that involve sex are more likely to be remembered the following day	❏	❏
Theft of stock and workplace materials tend to be less prevalent in departments in which employees are assigned clear, specific tasks rather than broad, vague roles	❏	❏
Solutions that are particularly novel are less likely to be criticised by management committees	❏	❏
Relative to other people, employees who are aware of their strengths and limitations tend to be more sociable and more impulsive	❏	❏
Middle managers are less likely to assume their CEO is effective and competent if this executive earns a moderate rather than an exorbitant salary	❏	❏
Individuals are less likely to donate money to charities if they are offered an inexpensive, futile gift in return, such as a sticker	❏	❏
Individuals are more likely to study diligently, avoid alcohol and retire early to bed the night before an important exam or meeting if they often feel a sense of anxiety, distress, or sadness at work	❏	❏
Employees who feel that everyone should question, rather than obey, authority and tradition are more likely to believe that other races are inferior	❏	❏
If employees watch a film that graphically depicts the disastrous consequences of exceeding the speed limit, they are less likely to speed in the future, provided they feel a sense of pride whenever they drive rapidly	❏	❏
Customers are more likely to be dissatisfied with the service they receive if they expect to be administered a survey that assesses their level of satisfaction	❏	❏
After managers receive rewards for fulfilling policies about discrimination and prejudice, they are less likely to exhibit discrimination or prejudice in the future	❏	❏

even further. Many managers have demonstrated great success despite these shortcomings. Imagine the success and talent they will manifest once these shortcomings are redressed.

Sources of Misconceptions

Why are many of our cherished, entrenched beliefs so misguided? Why do most individuals acquire so many misconceptions? Scientists have uncovered four principal sources of these misconceptions.

First, many of these misguided beliefs arise because the mental apparatus of humans is limited and subject to misconceptions of various kinds. The so-called *Sleeper Effect* represents an exemplary illustration of these limitations (see Lariscy & Tinkhm, 1999). To demonstrate, suppose that a prime minister alleged that the leader of the opposition emitted an unpleasant odour. The audience would recognise this contention as biased and therefore would perceive this assertion as tenuous. In other words, the audience would retain both the original assertion — that the leader of the opposition emits an unpleasant odour — as well as their belief this allegation is tenuous.

Over time, however, their belief this allegation is unsubstantiated would tend to dissolve from memory. Research demonstrates that the original allegation usually endures, even weeks after the scepticism towards this assertion fades. Eventually, only the assertion that the Leader of the Opposition emits an unpleasant odour will persist in their memory. A defect in the mental apparatus of humans — in this instance, the fragile memory of doubts — provokes a spate of erroneous beliefs.

Second, many misconceptions arise because of limitations in individuals' motivation (e.g., Haddock, 2002). When individuals reach decisions, they seldom feel motivated enough to consider every possible factor or alternative. Instead, they apply generic principles or rules to reach decisions. They select job applicants they like, rather than considering every skill and attribute. They purchase equipment that seems familiar, rather than analyse every feature and characteristic.

To illustrate, suppose you were asked to specify two favourable qualities that Winston Churchill demonstrated. Perhaps he might be perceived as assertive and cheerful or as realistic and confident. Because recognising two aspects is relatively easy, after you complete this exercise, you might unconsciously assume he probably displays many other desirable qualities as well. You are, therefore, likely to perceive him somewhat favourably (Haddock, 2002).

In contrast, suppose you were asked to specify five favourable qualities that Winston Churchill exhibited. Most individuals usually struggle to specify five favourable qualities of any person — they will not readily be able to divert their attention from the first two or three qualities they identified. As research indicates, you become more inclined to assume unwittingly that Winston Churchill presumably displayed few other desirable qualities. You may then perceive him unfavourably. In other words, managers often apply simple principles to evaluate other individuals or objects. These principles neglect vital information and thus yield biased evaluations.

Third, many misconceptions arise because our desires often contaminate our beliefs and opinions. For example, some managers crave power and influence; they prefer to assign specific tasks, activities and instructions to each employee, and this preference can distort their beliefs. They convince themselves erroneously that such behaviour is effective and appropriate and that employees become less focused, determined or productive when they do not receive specific goals from their supervisor. Research, however, shows that employees are more likely to squander resources, withhold cooperation, or behave dishonestly when they are assigned very specific goals from their supervisor (Levine & Jackson, 2002).

Finally, many misconceptions occur because managers receive either limited or distorted information. For example, managers are exposed to the opinions of only a segment of the population. Individuals who are especially influential —

leaders, politicians or consultants — are able to propel their beliefs and opinions throughout society more effectively. Managers are more likely, therefore, to encounter and thus espouse the opinions of influential individuals, but adopting these opinions provokes many misguided beliefs.

The experiences and subsequent insights of influential individuals do not necessarily apply to the entire population. Many influential management consultants, for example, have promoted the concept of a 'compliment sandwich', which maintains that all criticisms should be preceded and succeeded by praise. This strategy tends to improve responses to criticisms in confident, assured individuals — a quality of many influential consultants — but provoke resistance in everyone else (Brown, Farnham, & Cook, 2002). Influential individuals promulgated the compliment sandwich because this strategy applied to their demeanour.

Thus, many sources of bias contaminate our beliefs and opinions provoking unsuitable decisions. They will evaluate alternatives unfairly and will undertake their role ineffectively; eventually, their performance, confidence and status will decline. This book is intended to highlight and redress some of the misconceptions that reduce the effective performance of managers.

Readers who are now ready to challenge myths and misconceptions as well as accept advice have already progressed considerably. This willingness will enable you to implement behaviours, decisions and policies drawn from accurate scientific discoveries, rather than from instincts and intuition that often impair performance.

Chapter 2

Workplace Objectives

Promoting Workplace Values

One of the most disturbing misconceptions in management is demonstrated by the imposition of values and principles upon the workplace. Many large organisations have introduced a series of values and principles that employees must uphold and embrace. Through memoranda, presentations and meetings, employees may be implored to demonstrate integrity, safety, innovation, progress, performance and dedication. For example, the values of Intel, the world's largest manufacturer of microprocessor chips, include customer orientation, risk taking, discipline, results orientation, quality and a great place to work.

The reality revealed through research indicates organisations that urge employees to swear allegiance to these values tend to be less ethical and less effective (McKendall, DeMarr, & Jones-Rikkers, 2002). When organisations institute an official set of values, when they compel everyone to follow a series of prescribed ethical principles, employees become less likely to consider the outcomes of their behaviour. Instead, they tend to rely on official regulations to guide their behaviour. They follow all rules and policies, even if this behaviour could disadvantage other individuals. They become more likely to engage in acts previously regarded as unsuitable, immoral or unjust. If the organisation champions performance and sales, employees might lie to customers or ridicule the colleagues they disrespect because the organisation espouses openness and, therefore, provides an excuse to be offensive.

The evidence of this claim originated from a study that comprised two classes of organisations (McKendall, DeMarr, & Jones-Rikkers, 2002). The first had implemented a comprehensive program to promote ethics; they had instituted an ethics code, stipulating the principles that employees must uphold, and had provided extensive training in this code for all employees. The ethical behaviour of employees was also assessed and monitored closely and these evaluations determined pay, bonuses and promotions. The second organisation had not implemented a program to cultivate ethics. Those employees in organisations with an ethics program were actually more likely to behave inappropriately — they were more likely to breach policies and engage in acts that harm other individuals, such as violating safety regulations.

The imposition of values and principles reflects a second cherished misconception — that employees will adopt the attitudes the organisation promotes. Yet the findings show that, when employees feel compelled to express some attitude, promulgate some policy or impose some belief unto others, they become more likely to embrace a different position.

According to recent studies, individuals who are told to encourage safe practices become more likely to appreciate the benefits of risky behaviour (Maio & Olson, 1998). Individuals who are told to emphasise the importance of integrity will begin to recognise the value of deceit. Individuals who are told to instil cooperation and teamwork will begin to understand the importance of independence and competition. The values, desires, opinions and positions that employees strive to suppress gradually surface, intensify and magnify.

The reality is that employees become less likely to comply with workplace policies and regulations when the values their organisation espouses become too strict, too excessive or too ambitious. They perceive these policies as unduly conservative and unrealistic; regulations are seen as optional, arbitrary and unnecessary.

Once these misconceptions are recognised, several solutions can be introduced to ensure that employees conform to their own sense of morality, rather than follow regulations mechanically. First, managers should occasionally convene meetings where employees are encouraged to identify work-place behaviours they perceive as immoral but that comply with official codes or regulations. Examples may be the lunches designated as company expenses or the recruitment processes that disadvantage minorities. Individuals should then suggest tactics to discourage these behaviours without necessarily refining the official code.

Furthermore, managers should not enforce an official set of values or declare a series of principles that employees must embrace or accept. Instead, they should provide an environment where employees develop the skills and integrity to reach appro-priate decisions and engage in suitable behaviour themselves.

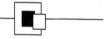

Managers should identify and then discourage workplace behaviours that seem unethical, even if they do not violate formal policies.

Creating a Company With a Vision and Inspiration

How should managers inspire their employees and ensure that they are driven to engage in suitable behaviours? To energise their workgroup, many managers now share their vision or image of the future. They convey the objectives they would like to achieve, the injustices they would like to address and the personal desires they would like to fulfil.

Some managers might aspire to invent a car that minimises pollution, to envisage elevator music that patrons would actually welcome or to devise a milk carton that can be opened from either side. Unfortunately, the impact of such visions tends to be short-lived. After several weeks, employees may revert to scepticism, ambivalence and gloom; their hopes might vanish and their performance may decline — they may become resistant to subsequent praise and affirmations. When employees are no longer inspired or optimistic, any endeavours to boost their performance with praise and approval may also diminish.

Why are these visions so impotent? First, many of these affirmations and visions are too specific. Managers incorrectly feel the need to specify the precise steps and actions they would like to realise. Yet they fail to suggest several inspiring goals or propose a few challenging, achievable targets. Instead, they stipulate each phase of their endeavour and delineate the specific activities they plan to undertake. 'First, we will employ three design engineers, two artists and four team leaders. Next, we will design a prototype to attract younger customers. Then, we will ...'

Research, however, demonstrates that visions involving an arrangement of specific tasks and targets do not inspire employees (Gonzales, Burgess, & Mobilo, 2001). As each target is proposed, employees become increasingly aware of all the obstacles, complications, impediments and aggravations they will need to overcome. Their initial sense of hope and exhilaration transforms into doubt, anxiety and cynicism; motivation vanishes and performance declines.

In a study supporting this effect (Gonzales, Burgess, & Mobilo, 2001), participants were asked to construct a plan that involved a sequence of specific, concrete activities — such as a decision to exclude dairy food, eat more vegetables, join a gym, begin exercise routines that last one hour and then extend these routines by 30 minutes after two weeks.

Some participants constructed a plan that comprised a few broad statements, such as the decision to engage in exercise at a gym and reduce calories. Individuals who constructed a plan with a sequence of specific, concrete activities were more likely to feel anxious rather than assured, weary rather than energetic and unmotivated rather than enthusiastic.

Other misconceptions may disrupt these visions. For example, many managers emphasise teamwork, collaboration and camaraderie so that the workgroup, and not the individuals, become the focal point of their vision. Employees perceive themselves as a collective, as an amalgam. This emphasis on collaboration and dependence, rather than on competition and independence, might seem an ideal.

Yet researchers have discovered some alarming problems that transpire in these work environments (Verplanken & Holland, 2002). A focus on teams rather than individuals can decimate, or at least diminish, the sensation of inspiration and drive that should follow the vision and affirmations of managers.

When individuals focus their attention towards the workgroup, disregarding their personal strengths, desires and burdens, they become less likely to fulfil their own values, principles and morals. They do not feel the burning desire to meet their instinctive standards for honesty, openness, safety, empathy, efficiency, or any of the other values they cherish. The values and principles they have acquired throughout their lifetimes become less likely to govern or drive their behaviour.

Instead, these employees follow only the values and principles upheld by their workgroup (Verplanken & Holland, 2002). Yet workgroups do not seem to demonstrate ethical values or follow scrupulous principles. Ethical, upright behaviours are seldom overt and thus generally overlooked, while egocentric, dishonest practices are more conspicuous and thus typically recognised. Employees may tend to follow the values and practices of their workgroup and engage in the insidious practices their colleagues often demonstrate.

Sometimes, managers will also need to announce a vision that could be unpopular, such as an initiative that entails retrenchments. Typically, managers aim to highlight the future benefits of this initiative, perhaps by claiming that the retrenchments will guarantee the sustainability of the organisation or that retrenchments will provide opportunities for promotion.

Research has revealed this inclination to emphasise benefits is hollow and risky (Shaw, Eric, & Colquitt, 2003). When managers highlight future benefits, they imply that alternative courses of action could have been pursued and that the decision was chosen, not imposed. Employees may therefore consider the prospect that some of these alternative options might have been more appropriate or more just and fair. Resentment soon grows and disloyalty develops.

Managers should therefore consider a series of solutions to amplify the impact of their vision. To magnify the impact of their vision, they should consider the injustices they would like to overcome such as establishing a second-hand car yard where the salespersons never fabricate or exaggerate. When managers promote a vision intended to redress an injustice, they inadvertently manifest a sense of passion — and even a trace of fury. These emotions have been demonstrated to enhance the force and impact of their vision (Lewis, 2000).

Second, before promoting this vision, managers should expose a few obstacles and complications that could hinder their endeavours, such as conservative executives, lobby groups or market forces and then identify some ways to surmount these issues. These activities can temper the doubt and alleviate managers' uncertainty. Managers who experience doubt and uncertainty, even subtly, tend to portray these concerns unwittingly through their facial expressions, posture, gestures and language (Bersen, Shamir, Avolio, & Popper, 2001). The audience senses this doubt and consequently feel uninspired or unimpressed.

Third, managers should assign a specific task to each employee before they present their vision. One employee could be asked to submit a press release about the ruses that employees use when selling cars; another employee could be encouraged to recruit another mechanic. Several weeks later, they could then highlight how all these tasks underpin a single inspiring vision. These specific tasks ensure the vision seems concrete, and these vivid images of the future have been shown to enhance optimism.

Finally, when managers need to announce an initiative that could be unpopular, such as retrenchments, they should demonstrate how factors beyond their control — such as government regulations or foreign exchange rates — precluded alternative courses of action, such as increased investment. Only afterwards should they highlight the future benefits of this initiative while conceding the primary drawbacks.

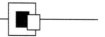

> *Managers should promote broad visions that overcome injustice. When they promulgate their vision, they should also describe some activities that are already underway or some goals that have already been achieved to advance these causes.*

Gaining Respect and Admiration

Two managers may proclaim the same vision, using the same words and same intonation, but only the manager who is perceived as credible and trustworthy and has earned respect and admiration will inspire their employees. Unfortunately, many managers do not know how to secure this respect and trust.

For example, when managers achieve some success, their behaviour usually undermines, rather than magnifies, the respect they receive. Many managers incorrectly believe they should subtly underscore their achievements by emphasising the clients they have secured, awards they have received and initiatives they have instituted.

Although implicit, they usually attribute their achievements to their innate, inherent qualities — their ability, insight, instincts and acumen. 'I simply followed my gut feeling' or 'My 15 years of experience served me well'. They do not credit these achievements to other factors they could not control, such as peer support, economic progress or fortune.

According to recent research, however, this omission forges a perception of arrogance rather than modesty, conceit rather than humility. Unlike their modest counterparts, conceited managers are assumed to possess few additional attributes and qualities — they promote cynicism, not admiration; odium rather than respect.

The ways managers respond in the aftermath of failure can also promote or diminish respect. When failures, shortfalls or errors arise in an organisation, managers may try to devolve their responsibility as a way to maintain their reputation. They may attempt to blame factors beyond their control — indolent employees, misguided executives, illness and misfortune.

Nevertheless, managers who do not blame themselves, assume no responsibility and fail to indicate how they could have acted differently, tend to be less admired. These managers are assumed to be unwilling or unable to prevent similar incidents in the future (Silvester, Anderson-Gough, Anderson, & Mohamed, 2002) and are presumed to be incompetent or unconfident.

As a way to earn more respect, some managers demonstrate the misconception that praise should be curbed. For example, in one IT company, rather than praise a group of employees, a manager distributed the following memorandum:

> I was disappointed to see a small group of folks staying late to move the office without the rest of the team. This would have been a short job if the whole group had pitched in and we could have saved additional billable time the next day.

Some managers may castigate their employees, undermine their executives, ridicule their customers and demonstrate the same lack of respect towards everyone else. They believe their derision towards other individuals is supposed to manifest their insight, their expertise and their talents.

Evidence indicates that managers who praise, rather than criticise, their employees are actually perceived as more credible and insightful (Davies, 1997). Criticisms are usually regarded as misguided and the source of this reproach is perceived as unintelligent or uninformed. By contrast, praise is usually (but unconsciously) regarded as perceptive and discerning — managers who confer this praise are perceived as astute and incisive.

In a study conducted in 1997, Martin Davies administered a personality inventory to participants who each received a summary of their personality that was supposedly derived from this instrument. In reality, each participant actually received the same description of their personality, including such generic phrases as 'You have a tendency to be critical of yourself'. The participants were then asked to rate the extent to which they believed each statement was an accurate portrayal of their character.

Most participants agreed with the statements that were favourable, such as 'Security is one of your major goals in life', but disagreed with the statements that were unfavourable, such as 'Some of your aspirations tend to be pretty unrealistic'. This study revealed that favourable statements inadvertently trigger the memory of events that verify this praise; hence, praise is usually perceived as accurate.

Whenever managers achieve some goal or outcome, they should identify obstacles that could have potentially precluded this success. In describing their feats to colleagues, managers should mention that they were fortunate that such obstacles did not emerge. For example, they could assert that the board had supported their initiatives or their staff had worked long hours. They should also indicate how they had been encouraged by peers to devote significant effort into this endeavour, recount some advice that had inspired their behaviour or relate some encouragement that had influenced their decisions.

Managers are more likely to be trusted and respected and to be perceived as confident but loyal, when they seem happy — rather than melancholy, anxious, frustrated or hostile. They should monitor their posture, gestures and appearance to convey a happy demeanour. Specifically, when sitting, their head and chest should be bent backwards; their arms should be straightened but slightly raised rather than placed along the side of their trunk (Coulson, 2004). Even physical aspects such as thick, bushy eyebrows can be unwittingly perceived to reflect hostility and frustration, rather than happiness and contentment, and should thus be trimmed (Montepare & Dobish, 2003).

To earn and retain respect, managers should concede their limitations as well as their achievements. Positive rather than negative feedback also enhances the prestige of managers. In addition, managers should practise gestures that have been demonstrated to promote admiration.

To further enhance credibility, managers need to illustrate or emphasise their arguments with gestures. When arguing that sales will soon grow, they should move their hands away from one another as they express this opinion. When they argue the incidence of injuries will contract, they should move their hands towards one another. Managers who exhibit these gestures have been demonstrated to seem more credible, more honest (Frank & Ehkman, 2004).

Finally, when employees express an idea, managers should identify and specify all the circumstances in which this proposal could be effective, rather than highlighting the potential obstacles. At least, they should not highlight these obstacles immediately but rather identify refinements that could accommodate these difficulties. Managers should veil their doubts, concerns and criticisms until after they have uncovered potential solutions to all of these issues. Indeed, research has revealed that managers who exhibit cynicism are perceived as more rigid and inflexible than managers who demonstrate optimism (Paglis & Green, 2002).

Assigning Roles to Employees

Once a manager has abolished the official set of values and principles; shown an inspiring, broad vision and direction; secured credibility and respect; as well as emphasised the strengths and qualities of each employee, they are ready to assign specific roles and tasks. For example, one employee may be instructed to prevent injuries, another will be encouraged to publicise the products and so forth.

However, managers often fail to assign roles appropriately. While they may claim to accommodate each individual's unique needs, concerns and attributes, few managers know how to fulfil this claim. For example, anxious, eccentric, unpredictable, unstable or awkward employees tend to be granted insignificant roles. These employees are not trusted and may be shielded from customers, suppliers and allies.

According to recent research, this approach fails to exploit the unique qualities of these individuals. Anxious individuals tend to feel tension and strain because they can anticipate potential obstacles and complications. They can foresee possible difficulties and problems (Stober, 1997). Therefore, anxious employees should be assigned roles that draw on their inclinations by allocating them to tasks that involve risk management or injury prevention.

Similarly, eccentric, unpredictable individuals are often rejected, shunned or dismissed. They seldom prevail during interviews and fail to flourish in organisations. Yet eccentric individuals can exhibit peculiar practices, express unique insights and can transcend the barriers of tradition or the constraints of convention (see, for example, O'Connor & Dyce, 2001). Hence, these individuals should be involved in creative solutions to problems that seem untenable.

Unstable, awkward employees also tend to exhibit some unique qualities. These employees may not appear to manage their emotions effectively, seeming sensitive, emotional, impulsive or unpredictable, rather than understanding, empathic or supportive towards others. A project conducted by Wong and

Law (2002) determined that even these individuals have unique strengths and benefits. They are more likely to persist and remain in jobs that involve minimal interaction, to exhibit commitment towards jobs that involve working with limited companionship or communication.

Managers also tend to assign simple tasks to those employees they regard as being unproductive, unskilled, untried and undisciplined; whereas difficult and challenging activities are confined to effective, astute individuals. This practice, however, defies some important scientific discoveries. When employees receive difficult, challenging tasks, their performance typically exceeds their expectations (Windschitl, Kruger, & Nus Simms, 2003) and their motivation and productivity rises. For example, studies have shown that most participants believe they will answer more general-knowledge questions than other individuals if the topic seems simple, such as 1980s music. Conversely, they believe that, if the topic seems difficult, such as the Byzantine empire, they will answer fewer general-knowledge questions than other individuals. Most participants believe they would not exceed the average level of performance, yet half these individuals would exceed the average, despite the relative obscurity of this topic.

Managers can display even more profound misconceptions when they assign roles to individuals who are sociable, gregarious, assertive and extraverted — rather than to those who are reserved, unconfident and feeble. Sociable, assertive employees usually receive roles that involve leadership and responsibility, such as project management, coordination, authority, administration, influence and guidance of other individuals. Yet these individuals are not usually suited to these roles as they seldom exhibit enough insight into themselves or others to fulfil these roles effectively. Specifically, scientists have revealed that extraverted, gregarious individuals seldom ponder or reflect upon the events that transpire and therefore often interpret events incorrectly (Fletcher & Baldry, 2000).

To illustrate this point, when they receive praise, they do not consider the purpose of the feedback and fail to recognise the praise was manipulative rather than genuine. When a colleague seems upset, they do not consider the source of this mood and are less aware of their faults, their limitations and their impact. They may not recognise the possibility that some of their own behaviour was responsible and may misconstrue the intentions of their colleagues.

Fletcher and Baldry (2000) conducted a research study in which employees were asked to rate themselves and one another on their behaviour at work. For example, they assessed the extent to which employees initiated improvements, forged relationships, enhanced teamwork and so on. Individuals who were sociable, rather than reserved, were significantly more likely to overrate themselves — their perception of their own behaviour did not align with the evaluations of their colleagues.

Similarly, executives tend to seek managers who are assertive, commanding and assured. They prefer managers who can reach and implement unpopular decisions and who are perceived as firm but fair — however science suggests otherwise. Leaders who are assertive and dominating can provoke consequential, damaging workplace issues. Employees and leaders will not always adopt the same opinions and beliefs and may differ in their attitudes towards integrity, or their emphasis on safety. Usually, employees are not too perturbed when they discover this disparity and accept leaders with opinions that differ from their own.

However, this acceptance can transform into resentment and distress if the leader exhibits an assertive, commanding persona (Mills, Cooper, & Forest, 2002). These leaders can be perceived as influential and powerful, and these employees will feel especially threatened. They feel particularly vulnerable in response to a leader's divergent attitude. Because of this apprehension, these employees may attempt to undermine such leaders and will convince themselves these leaders are unworthy, incompetent and impotent.

Similarly, managers should not assign all roles that involve leadership to males, despite males being perceived as superior leaders in almost every workplace. They are thought to earn more respect as a leader — but, is this respect warranted? Recent studies suggest that males and females who are equally assertive, decisive, intelligent, resilient and persuasive still do not receive the same respect (Jackson, Esses, & Burris, 2001). Thus, males receive more respect because they tend to receive positions of authority — a consequence of patriarchal traditions that pervade most societies.

So, managers should not assign positions of responsibility only to males as this tendency would reflect a distorted perception of females. Such an allocation of responsibility would not utilise the qualities of female employees.

Managers should consider not only the qualities of the consummate leader, but also the context. For example, perhaps a manager would like to introduce a new leader from outside the group into a particular team, but the previous leader remains. This practice might seem reasonable, but an obvious tension could eventuate. Studies indicate that, in this type of situation, members of a team usually support one individual or the other. They may defend the practices, policies and customs of the previous regime or champion the initiatives and proposals of the new leader. The team becomes political, partisan, wary, guarded and thus unproductive (Worchel, Jenner, & Hebl, 1998).

Finally, managers may devolve too much responsibility to their employees by trying to delegate too many tasks and roles. Perhaps they may have read articles or heard experts promoting the importance of delegation and how it can foster their employees' development and confidence as well as promote efficiency. Delegation is also promoted as a way to curtail the manager's own workload.

But, scientists now recognise that this obsession with delegation does not enhance workplace performance nor alleviate the feelings of stress that pervade the workplace. Instead, research reveals that undue delegation promotes a sense of incompetence in employees who do not feel equipped to fulfil their responsibilities (Sigler & Pearson, 2000). They feel overloaded with demands and difficulties and do not understand these feelings are ubiquitous or inevitable. They may perceive themselves as inadequate and unsuited to leadership and thus shun positions of responsibility in the future and limit their development.

So, how can managers assign roles appropriately? As discussed, individuals who are anxious should be assigned roles that involve risk management, such as injury prevention. Individuals who are eccentric and unpredictable should be assigned roles that involve creative solutions to problems that seem untenable. Individuals who are assertive, commanding and confident should be assigned fewer subordinates rather than large teams. Managers should ensure these subordinates share similar values and opinions to their assertive leaders. One drawback of the uniformity of these workgroups is that it tends to stifle creativity, originality and novelty; so these leaders should not manage teams that are formed to promote innovation.

Second, managers should also consider the facial characteristics of employees in respect to their roles. In some jobs, employees must convince other individuals to be cooperative or charitable; perhaps they might need to seek donations from customers. Other employees might need to seek approval from government bodies to undertake some project. Research indicates that employees with large eyes, thick lips, thin eyebrows and a narrow jaw line are especially likely to be effective in these jobs (Keating, Randall, Kendrick, & Gutshall, 2003). These features are ubiquitous in young children and thus denote innocence, honesty, compassion. Employees with these features are more likely to be trusted than other individuals.

Third, all individuals must experience a transition period as a team member before they are given any authority or leadership. Once they receive this authority, they should not challenge the previous leader immediately or provoke division. They should not eradicate traditional practices or introduce innovative operations. Instead, they should focus their attention towards the support of colleagues, at least during the first month or so.

Fourth, managers should assign a few difficult, challenging tasks to employees who are not especially confident or effective, while emphasising that these tasks are complex and demanding. Typically, employees will perform more effectively than anticipated, which subsequently boosts their confidence, their motivation and their productivity.

After they receive appropriate training, seemingly unmotivated, unskilled, or unproductive employees should be encouraged to undertake some difficult, demanding activities that utilise their unique qualities.

Finally, delegation must coincide with additional training. Employees must be encouraged to understand that the stress they now feel — the demands they currently experience — will fade as their training proceeds.

Employee Goal Setting

Once roles have been assigned, managers must then allocate specific goals to employees. Perhaps one employee might be asked to complete two tender proposals by next week or to secure three new accounts. When managers do not prescribe specific goals, targets and instructions, employees feel impotent rather than empowered. By contrast, when managers prescribe specific goals, targets and instructions, their employees might feel frustrated or invaded rather than trusted and respected.

The preference of many managers is to prescribe concrete goals, set precise targets and present specific instructions. They may specify the order in which activities should be completed, the methods to be used and the effort that needs to be expended.

Despite the popularity of this approach, science has uncovered many sobering insights (Strickland & Galimba, 2001). When managers prescribe very specific goals and targets, they may fail to communicate some important details — such as the precise order in which these tasks should be completed. The employees must thus uncover these details themselves while they complete the activities. They may then need to consider adjustments to their strategy; perhaps they will begin to feel uncertain and appear distracted.

In one research program that highlighted these complications, participants performed a series of tasks. Some were prescribed clear targets — for example, they might have been instructed to complete at least ten arithmetic problems — while others were not prescribed clear targets. Interestingly, participants who were prescribed clear targets tended to switch their attention frequently and sporadically between tasks — a strategy that tends to impair productivity and performance (Strickland & Galimba, 2001).

In some organisations, managers encourage employees to set their own goals and invite them to impose their own deadlines to foster motivation and minimise procrastination. Unfortunately, several careful research studies indicate this approach does not promote motivation or productivity as effectively as the deadlines imposed by supervisors (Ariely & Wertenbroch, 2002). For example, the duration that employees devote to each task should primarily depend on the time needed to complete these activities. To proofread three papers of equal length in 15 days, no more than five days should be dedicated to each article. Many employees, however, devote less time to tasks they will undertake in the future. They might dedicate 6 days to the first article, 5 days to the second article and 4 days to the final article. This tendency arises because employees do not attach enough importance to future stress and are more concerned with immediate discomfort, rather than future needs.

Similarly, to promote productivity and foster motivation, managers often encourage employees to set many subgoals. Rather than impose a broad, remote objective — such as 'Create an engaging advertising campaign' — they set a series of specific, concrete, manageable subgoals, such as 'This week, identify the target audience', 'Next week, determine the message this commercial will portray'. These subgoals can indeed promote motivation and enthusiasm in some contexts, in some employees.

But unfortunately, some sophisticated studies have shown these subgoals should not be applied when employees need to propose creative solutions and ideas, as they may block originality and deter innovation. Specifically, when employees receive a series of subgoals, they focus upon their immediate duties and obligations and seldom consider their future aspirations.

Images of the future, however, have been demonstrated to promote novel suggestions and creative solutions (Forster, Friedman, & Liberman, 2004). After employees imagine events that might arise in the distant future, perhaps one year from now, they spontaneously focus upon broad, abstract concepts rather than specific, concrete objects or activities. For example, while they observe a conflict, they might focus upon the abstract, underlying objectives of each party — their latent desires, underlying apprehensions or philosophical doctrines — and not the specific remarks. This emphasis on broad, abstract concepts has been demonstrated to foster creative, original suggestions.

Thus, managers should set subgoals for only a circumscribed set of employees rather that applying the same approach to every employee, regardless of their preferences, temperament, experience, responsibilities and so forth. Many personality characteristics influence the performance of employees after they set their own targets (Tsuzuki & Matsui, 1998). For example, some employees are disciplined, methodical and organised at work and thus feel inspired and earnest when they receive concrete goals and targets. Hence, they prefer managers who impose specific goals.

By contrast, employees who are not diligent and methodical like their work to involve spontaneous activities, unexpected events and sufficient autonomy. Managers who prescribe concrete goals inhibit this spontaneity, frustrate these employees and thus impair their commitment and performance.

Furthermore, in some workgroups, each employee is instructed to pursue several goals and tasks concurrently — they might be asked to prepare some document, then to resolve some customer complaint, analyse some data, sort various files or complete some other fleeting activity. This system, however, has been demonstrated to curb productivity in many circumstances (Slocombe & Bluedorn, 1999). Some employees prefer to begin one task only after they have completed the previous activity and may experience considerable stress when managers prescribe several goals and targets concurrently. In particular, these employees will strive to override their ingrained inclination to complete tasks in sequence by attempting to pursue several objectives simultaneously. Dismissing their preferences may induce stress, disquiet, resentment and ultimately withdrawal and inefficiency.

Many managers also encourage employees to set themselves challenging, ambitious or onerous goals. To satisfy their managers, employees might resolve to write five reports, send ten emails and telephone fifteen clients over the ensuing week. Unfortunately, unexpected issues arise when employees strive to achieve challenging goals. Employees tend to underestimate the time needed to complete activities, especially if these tasks are repetitive and have been practised extensively (see Yarmey, 2000). Because of this distorted estimate, they believe they will be able to complete more activities within a specific timeframe than is actually possible — thus they may become disillusioned when they fail to achieve another goal.

Daniel Yarmey (2000) asked participants to complete a series of activities, such as operate an ATM, purchase a train ticket, read an article and so forth. Participants were asked to estimate the duration of these activities in advance, but the actual time taken almost invariably exceeded their estimates. This finding has been replicated in many other studies.

This underestimation is especially pronounced when the task involves repetitive actions. That is, when individuals estimate the duration of a task, they primarily consider the phase in which they devise and plan the activities — so the time to complete tasks involving minimal planning is substantially underestimated. To exacerbate this issue, employees typically experience significant distress and disappointment when they fail to achieve the goals they set (Coughlan & Connolly, 2001). Indeed, in one study, participants were asked to estimate the level of performance they believed they could reach on some task. Before they engaged in this activity, they predicted the magnitude of displeasure they would experience if they were not able to achieve this level of performance. After completing this activity, their level of displeasure experienced was assessed if they failed to achieve their target. Most participants experienced significantly more displeasure than they had anticipated — feeling more disillusioned, alarmed, helpless or ashamed. Such displeasure destroys their motivation, drive and optimism in the future.

Fortunately, many of these obstacles can be overcome. First, employees should be asked to set their own goals and targets, either alone or together with their manager, who should ensure these goals and targets are applicable. The manager's role encompasses verifying that employees formulate goals utilising their skills, encouraging them to undertake roles their colleagues do not want to fulfil. The manager should also ensure that employees perform tasks that will advance their expertise, but set targets that are not unduly challenging.

Second, employees should be encouraged to estimate the time they will need to devote to some task or activity before they begin, perhaps by recording how long they will need to write some report, analyse some data, catalogue some files, proofread some article and so forth. It is also beneficial to then record the actual duration of each task. Comparisons between predicted and actual durations can be illuminating and can enhance the ability of employees to plan their schedules.

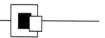

> *Employees should be involved in setting their goals and targets, which should be specified explicitly and expressed aloud on several occasions. Whenever they set these goals and targets, they should also include some discretionary activities — that is, tasks that are optional but beneficial.*

Unfortunately, employees do not always realise their goals and intentions, whether personal or work-related. To increase this likelihood they should aim to fulfil their intention to a moderate extent, then express their intention — aloud but alone — twice a day over the course of a week. After this week, they should strive to fulfil their intention. Intentions and goals that are concrete in employees' memory are more likely to be realised. Intentions become more concrete and prominent if they are expressed on several occasions or if they have been achieved in the past (Cooke & Sheeran, 2004).

Despite making these changes, individuals may still formulate unrealistic plans, set implausible schedules and targets or fail to realise their deadlines. It is useful to incorporate a buffer in one's plans; some time for discretionary activities. Perhaps the plan could include a phase in which employees identify activities that were frustrating or in which tasks that did not contribute to the final product are uncovered. Regardless, employees should strive to complete these discretionary activities before the deadline is reached. If necessary, these discretionary activities could be postponed if the deadline is not fulfilled.

Chapter 3

Team Performance

Collaborating Across Different Workgroups

As illustrated in the previous chapter, managers need to communicate an inspiring vision, assign suitable roles and then encourage employees to formulate appropriate goals and targets. These measures will guarantee some improvement in *workgroup* performance; but they may not necessarily guarantee a concurrent improvement in *workplace* performance. The performance of organisations improves only if the workgroups integrate effectively, where various departments or teams unite.

Workgroups do not always cohere effectively; they might neglect, contest, distrust, sabotage or deceive one another. Even though they may seem to operate in harmony, the demands and concerns of others may be disregarded or misconstrued — few managers appreciate the factors that can provoke this dissonance.

One of the most subtle, but vital, sources of this discord can arise from the biases of managers. Some managers believe activities of their own department are more consequential and complex than the activities of other departments (Jetten, Spears, & Manstead, 1997). They perceive their own workgroup as more advanced, more sophisticated or more important. As a consequence, they believe their department deserves more resources, assistance and attention from the organisation to ensure they can fulfil their potential. Accordingly, such managers may not strive to support other workgroups, but consider that other workgroups should support them instead.

Some managers develop this bias towards their own workgroup to bolster their pride and confidence. When their own workgroup encounters some difficulty — perhaps a decline in sales or a rise in costs — managers unwittingly identify unavoidable factors that might have exacerbated these issues, such as economic decline, executive decisions or market fluctuations. But, according to recent studies, they do not extend this courtesy to other workgroups (Gardham & Brown, 2001), instead noticing every flaw, shortfall or problem in rival departments.

Disharmony across workgroups does not stem exclusively from this bias. Each workgroup usually emphasises different values, needs and objectives. Perhaps the manufacturing department may underscore product quality or production expenses, while the sales department may underscore product range or delivery speed. Departments will adopt their own values to evaluate other workgroups and thus may perceive one another as ineffective, misguided or inflexible. Researchers have revealed that this problem leads to situations where trust vanishes, negotiations stall and collaborations cease (Nauta, De Dreu, & Der Vaart, 2002).

A few organisations have already attempted to foster collaboration across workgroups and departments by ensuring that the bonuses each workgroup receives depend on the performance of departments to which they provide services. Research and development is rewarded if the marketing department is successful; the engineering department is rewarded if the manufacturing division is more productive. Suddenly, these workgroups fulfil standards they had never previously attained and value facets of performance they had never pursued before. These initiatives, however, have been shown to exacerbate resentment; specifically, these initiatives have been shown to provoke unfair blame — especially when goals are not realised.

In other organisations, the various workgroups evaluate one another. They assess the extent to which they regard the other workgroups as cooperative, insightful, prompt, sincere and so forth. Only workgroups that are evaluated favourably receive bonuses; yet surprisingly, these initiatives have been shown to actually impede progress (Ayers, Dahlstrom, & Skinner, 1997). While they may foster cooperation, they do not promote debate or deliberation. Departments become reluctant to confront, challenge and question one another. Progress may be stifled and problems remain unresolved.

A variety of other strategies have also been applied to foster collaboration. For example, managers often attempt to prevent discord between various departments by avoiding any form of competition between various workgroups or units. They would never organise a trivia night in which two separate workgroups compete, nor organise a football match between two distinct departments. Instead, each team would comprise members of both workgroups or departments. This sensitivity, according to several insightful studies, is unfounded (Chan & Ybarra, 2002); instead, competitions foster admiration towards rivals and competitions promote respect.

Employees tend to inadvertently overestimate the strengths and qualities of rivals — and trivialise the limitations and shortfalls of these opponents — to prevent disappointment with the outcome. They might, for example, remember and focus their attention towards information that highlights the strengths of their rivals and disregard information regarding the limitations. Research reveals that employees would seldom remember a rival who asserts, 'I arrived late because I was hung over', because this remark emphasises a limitation. By contrast, they often remember a rival who asserts, 'I arrived late because my alarm clock was faulty', because this remark does not emphasise a personal limitation.

Likewise, organisations sometimes need to foster collaboration amongst workgroups whose roles are entirely different, such as sales and engineering. In these instances, some managers strive to merge or blend or fuse the workgroups by attempting to diminish the boundaries or demarcations that separate them. Perhaps the employees in each workgroup are shifted to the same work area, or business cards may not specify whether they operate in the sales or marketing workgroup.

Experts now recognise this approach is unwise as it fosters disdain towards the other workgroup. It can provoke disrespect towards the colleagues with whom these employees are supposed to collaborate (Jetten, Spears, & Postmes, 2004). To illustrate, in some organisations, the workgroups are distinct, discrete and demarcated and employees derive a sense of attachment, pride and confidence from their workgroup. However, in other organisations, workgroups may be hazy and employees cannot obtain this bonding from their workgroup. In an attempt to boost their pride and bolster their confidence, they may perceive their attributes, experiences and responsibilities as superior. Subsequently, they inadvertently lack respect for individuals whose attributes, experiences and responsibilities are entirely different from those of their own team.

To reconcile these issues and promote collaboration, a series of recommendations should be considered. The workgroups' bonuses should first depend on both the performance and evaluations of other departments. To illustrate, workgroups should receive some bonus if the departments to which they provide products and services reach some criterion or goal. For instance, resources and development should receive some bonus if the marketing department fulfils some target.

However, the bonus should be retracted if this workgroup is not perceived as cooperative, insightful, prompt, sincere and so forth — the various workgroups should evaluate one another on these attributes. Only workgroups that are evaluated favourably should be eligible to receive bonuses.

Second, managers should identify the extent to which each department emphasises aspects such as product quality, production expenses, product range, delivery speed, innovation or customer service. Managers should then identify workgroups that do not emphasise some value to the same extent as do other departments. These workgroups should be rewarded if their performance on these values improves in the future.

> *Collaboration between teams and departments that are somewhat similar to one another should be fostered. Specifically, these workgroups should receive bonuses if they cooperate and assist one another. The boundaries between workgroups should also be obscured. Competition between teams and departments that are essentially different to one another should be encouraged.*

Third, employees should be rotated to other workgroups and departments as these experiences can promote empathy, respect and collaboration (Parker & Axtell, 2001). Other measures can also be implemented to exploit the benefits of this exposure and the effects of these experiences.

Parker and Axtell (2001) found that employees who have been rotated to several areas begin to appreciate the unique complications, understand the inherent obstacles and sympathise with the difficulties of other individuals, workgroups and departments. They recognise that subtle, insidious impediments hinder every employee. After several rotations, they learn to accept and respect other individuals, even the employees with whom they had not collaborated.

Finally, organisations sometimes need to encourage cooperation amongst disparate workgroups, such as sales and engineering. In these instances, they should ensure that employees feel a sense of attachment or bond to their own workgroup — perhaps their business cards should specify the workgroup in which they belong. Perhaps they should promote some competition between these workgroups.

To illustrate, employees from a variety of workgroups could attend the same training program where some incentive in the form of a reward or bonus is offered to the workgroup that demonstrates the most pronounced improvement in their knowledge, expertise and skills. Interactions before competitions with employees from other workgroups or departments tend to foster respect and admiration, rather than disdain or contempt, towards one another.

Yet this strategy should not be pursued when organisations need to foster collaboration amongst workgroups whose roles are similar, such as sales and marketing. In these instances, managers should not differentiate the workgroups too often.

Team Cohesion

Conflicts, disputes and discord are not restricted to individuals in rival workgroups as disharmony can also be common between individuals in the same workgroup. Some managers invest exorbitant sums of money to foster teamwork and cooperation by drawing on experts and consultants to eradicate discord and promote harmony. Employees engage in programs, games, exercises and adventures that are intended to instil trust, empathy and cooperation — but is this harmony so important? Is teamwork really effective? Many studies now reveal that teamwork does not always enhance the performance of workgroups. While unmitigated conflict and resentment is destructive, unmitigated *cooperation* can also impair performance (e.g., Houghton, Simon, Aquino, & Goldberg, 2000). Most managers would like all discussions to feature cooperation, compromise, trust, respect and naïve optimism rather than conflict or disagreement.

When individuals operate and cooperate in a team environment, their ability, concentration and ingenuity all tend to decline. Vital factors and considerations are neglected in their attempt to formulate plans and reach decisions (Houghton, Simon, Aquino, & Goldberg, 2000). Their plans, decisions and performance are thus compromised. These shortcomings arise because the cues and strategies they usually apply to recall facts, retrieve information and remember details are disrupted in team settings.

Furthermore, these individuals feel motivated, even obliged, to focus their attention upon factors and issues they all understand. They do not want to demonstrate disrespect towards team members with facts their colleagues have not encountered, nor to intimidate other team members with knowledge their colleagues have not acquired. Expertise, knowledge and insights that reside in the minds of only one or two individuals have been shown to be disregarded. Accordingly, individuals should first construct their ideas, solutions and opinions alone before they share and refine these suggestions in a team environment.

These complications were highlighted in a systematic, insightful series of studies (e.g., Houghton, Simon, Aquino, & Goldberg, 2000) where participants were asked to evaluate a revolutionary product — contact lenses for chickens. They read feedback from potential customers to decide whether or not this product should be pursued and were then asked to justify this decision. Participants could work either in teams or alone. When participants operated in teams, they committed more errors in logic. Criticisms from one or two customers tended to influence their decision unduly in that they incorrectly assumed that problems in one particular condition were also likely to emerge in other circumstances. When participants operated alone, they were less likely to demonstrate these logical flaws.

Indeed, team cohesion has been shown to curb the drive or incentive of employees (White, Sanbonmatsu, Croyle, & Smittipatana, 2002). Team members who feel compassion, empathy and warmth towards one another do not want to outperform each other or to expose the limitations, shortfalls or weaknesses of individuals they like. So, they may bridle their enthusiasm and performance, thus containing their effort and passion.

Fortunately, this tendency can be prevented. If the productivity of workgroups — rather than individuals — is assessed to determine bonuses, employees become more reluctant to outperform their colleagues (White et al., 2002). Indeed, in many organisations, workgroups that fulfil their responsibilities, transcend their targets and outperform other teams receive significant bonuses and rewards.

But, this emphasis on workgroup, rather than individual, productivity has also been shown to provoke some unforseen problems (Guthrie, 2000). It can hinder motivation and effort, especially in unmotivated, unconfident and manipulative employees who may perceive this scheme as an opportunity to conserve energy, to reduce effort.

By contrast, some organisations do not reward effective teams, workgroups and departments. While effective employees might receive promotions and effective managers might receive bonuses, effective teams receive no formal rewards or recognition.

Team cohesion can mitigate many workplace issues and promote satisfaction. When individuals feel a sense of attachment, loyalty, identity and bond towards their team, they become less concerned with their own status and conditions. For instance, they become less likely to feel dissatisfied with their remuneration (Wheeler, 2002). In addition, anxiety is less likely to incite antagonism and hostility when the individuals feel attached to their team. Distress is less likely to provoke aggression when the individuals feel bonded to their workgroup. Throughout evolution, individuals who act aggressively in collectives are less likely to receive support from peers and thus unlikely to survive. So, natural selection has eradicated the tendency to exhibit hostility in team settings (Twenge, Baumeister, Tice, & Stucke, 2000).

Provided that individuals initially pursue solutions, suggestions and ideas alone and that workgroup productivity is emphasised more than individual performance, team cohesion and allegiance becomes a powerful force. But, can this cohesion be cultivated? Can this sense of identity be fostered? Research has identified some important factors that promote attachment and commitment to the work-group. For example, teams tend to become more cohesive, empathic and supportive when each member receives some training in the role of their colleagues (Cannon-Bowers, Salas, Blickensderfer, & Bowers, 1998).

But team cohesion cannot be cultivated or developed if the raw ingredients are lacking and key obstacles are not avoided. Managers often strive to form teams of employees who exhibit similar traits, tendencies and temperaments, although research has highlighted the futility of this practice. A workgroup that comprises only sociable, extraverted, commanding individuals does not function effectively. Similarly, a team of reserved, introverted members also tends to be less productive and efficient. Teams tend to be most productive, satisfied and cohesive when the members do not all exhibit the same personality or character — when the members are not all gregarious or all reserved (Neuman, Wagner, & Christiansen, 1999).

Furthermore, managers' feedback can also influence the cohesion of teams. To encourage and motivate workgroups, managers may use dire predictions and strident criticisms. They inform teams that performance, efficiency, motivation and attitudes must improve or may threaten them with the prospect of demotions, retrenchments and other penalties.

This approach, however, is more destructive than even the most cynical manager would envisage (Bachrach, Bendoly, & Podsakoff, 2001). Specifically, this approach reduces coopera-tion, collaboration and attachment. Most employees have developed their own beliefs in relation to the qualities that enhance workgroup performance. They usually believe coop-erative, supportive colleagues will improve the performance of workgroups. So, when employees are told their workgroup has performed ineffectively or that their team has not fulfilled its objectives, they assume their colleagues have not exhibited these traits. They assume their colleagues have been uncooper-ative, unsupportive, or nonempathic and these assumptions dissolve team cohesion.

One study that exemplifies this behaviour involved participants being assigned to teams where they had to complete some task that involved interaction and discussion. After the completed these tasks, some of the teams were told they had performed inefficiently, regardless of their actual performance. Other teams were told they had performed superbly. After they received this feedback, each participant was asked to anonymously rate the extent to which they perceived the other team members as cooperative and supportive. Teams that were told they had performed inefficiently rated their colleagues as uncooperative rather than supportive and obliging (Bachrach, Bendoly, & Podsakoff, 2001).

To cultivate team cohesion appropriately, each member should first be granted the opportunity to develop some unique skills, insights and knowledge. They should then be encouraged to impart some of this expertise to their colleagues. Over time, this exercise has been demonstrated to promote team cohesion, respect and trust.

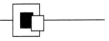

To promote team cohesion, managers should introduce some unusual or unique activity each month — an activity that all employees experience together.

Second, some research (Jaussi & Dionne, 2003) has suggested that, each week, managers should engage in some unconventional behaviour or activities to promote team cohesion. This might involve standing on a chair when convening a discussion, asking employees to wear T-shirts that specify their goals and targets that week, or to write some memorandum in crayons. Employees who experience an unusual event together — such as an unconventional manager — tend to feel a sense of attachment to each other.

Promoting Employee Performance and Reducing Anxiety

Inspiration, motivation and thus productivity will rise if employees feel attached, bonded and dedicated to their team. Yet employees will only feel this attachment and dedication if performance is elevated. So, can managers promote performance without first improving inspiration, motivation and cohesion? Yes, they can.

Many managers do not recognise that every characteristic of the work environment can influence performance and productivity. For example, most managers permit employees to attach posters or prints to the walls of their office — such as a picture of surfers at the beach or a photograph of their friends at a party. Indeed, attempts to prohibit these pictures would seem draconian and would probably be condemned.

Yet these pictures can dramatically influence the productivity and behaviour of employees (Banfield, Pendry, Mewse, & Edwards, 2003). For example, photographs of surfers — particularly unknown surfers — activate mental, unconscious images of the characteristics that are associated with these individuals. These photographs might activate memories of relaxation or frivolity or rebellion — images that tend to disrupt motivation, dedication and thus performance.

To illustrate this point, in several studies, participants received a photograph of an elderly stranger. Immediately afterwards, these participants became more likely to exhibit the stereotypical behaviour of elderly citizens (e.g., Banfield, Pendry, Mewse, & Edwards, 2003) by walking more slowly and gingerly or adopting more conservative attitudes and so forth (Kawakami, Dovidio, & Dijksterhuis, 2003).

Some managers encourage employees to attach pictures of a specific, renowned individual, such as Albert Einstein, Weary Dunlop or Nelson Mandela. They believe that such pictures might inculcate employees with the qualities of these inspiring individuals. Yet some research indicates that pictures of a renowned and inspiring individual can actually impair performance. In one study, for example, some participants observed a photograph of Albert Einstein while others observed a photograph of a celebrated supermodel (Haddock, Macrae, & Fleck, 2002). Relative to the other participants, individuals who observed Einstein performed less effectively on a test that assesses general knowledge. These individuals tended to focus on the differences between themselves and Albert Einstein. They felt unintelligent in comparison — their motivation and confidence declined and their memory and performance deteriorated.

Unfortunately, few managers recognise the factors that can influence performance or recognise that it can be improved without the need to instil pressure, promote drive or demand cooperation. Many managers urge their employees to strive more vigorously and work more energetically, yet these appeals do not enhance productivity or efficiency. However, concentration diminishes whenever employees feel anxious, tense, strained. Anxiety activates regions in the brain called the 'right prefrontal region' and individuals are less able to focus on specific details and objects within a complex environment (Moore & Oaksford, 2002). They tend to overlook important cues and signals.

In addition, when employees feel tense and agitated they try to prevent errors, by working cautiously. But this cautious, circumspect approach does not enhance performance and usually impedes their development and inhibits their improvement. By trying to prevent errors they do not explore novel strategies nor do they experiment with various methods and techniques. Their expertise does not grow and their performance does not improve.

To substantiate this argument, Stanley Gully and his colleagues (2002) published an important research program in which participants learned how to perform a task that involved tracking objects with radar. Some of the participants were encouraged to commit errors intentionally while they practised this task. For example, they were informed that committing errors can facilitate the learning process. Other participants were informed that committing errors could impede their ability to learn. Relative to the other individuals, participants who were encouraged to commit errors tended to learn and perform this task more effectively.

Prolonged anxiety and stress can also promote fatigue and exhaustion, which can impair performance, especially on repetitive tasks — such as driving a car, working on a production line or monitoring a radar screen. Usually, these tasks are predictable and uneventful but the demands can suddenly change. Suddenly, a hazard can appear — pedestrians, police cars, road works, snow; the fatigued driver or the exhausted operator, must adjust their effort to become alert, vigilant and focused.

Their fatigue prevents this adaptation, even if they are otherwise disciplined and motivated, by preventing an upsurge in concentration and effort. They might be able to override feelings of fatigue momentarily, with gushing air or blaring music but they cannot override their inability to adjust their effort (Desmond & Matthews, 1997). This anxiety partly arises from the systems of performance appraisal and assessment. In many organisations, individuals receive bonuses, promotion, or recognition if they outperform their colleagues. Perhaps, the five most productive employees will receive a bonus. Scientists have shown that individuals who try to outperform colleagues do not concentrate effectively. They experience distractions and worry as well as tension and anxiety (Linnenbrink, Ryan, & Pintrich, 2000).

There are many misconceptions relating to the level of anxiety that employees experience. For example, some individuals believe they should not reflect upon their problems before they retire to bed, assuming that this deliberation will disturb their sleep. Yet, research suggests this assumption hinders a vital source of personal development and progress (White & Taytroe, 2003). Employees may form an image of a problem before they retire to bed — perhaps envisaging a dispute with a friend or a shortfall in their confidence.

If they then repeat the phrase, 'How can I solve this dilemma?' or 'How can I address this problem?' for several minutes they will often experience dreams in which they attempt ways to resolve this issue. These dreams, even if not recalled the following morning, will nevertheless offer some insights into their problems. They will foster a sense of clarity and provide a sense of confidence. Anxiety will dissipate and their distress will diminish.

Anxiety also depends on the values and objectives the organisation adopts. Even the manufacturing strategy of organisations can influence anxiety and thus performance. Every organisation strives to reduce costs, enhance quality, streamline delivery and foster flexibility. But, these objectives may often conflict with one another, requiring executives to emphasise one or two goals over others. They might stress the importance of quality and flexibility or emphasise quality and delivery. The majority of organisations, however, emphasise low costs and high quality.

Research indicates that this emphasis provokes some critical problems (Kathuria, 2000). Costs can be monitored more readily than quality, thus organisations focus more on costs than quality, albeit unwittingly. They attempt to stream-line processes, rather than improve the reliability of their products. They aim to downsize the organisation, rather than augment the durability of goods. In other words, they prima-rily focus on internal operations, not customer needs, leading to the decline in the performance and reputation of these organisations. Employees become anxious and uneasy as they experience conflicting demands.

Similarly, an emphasis on cost reduction typically augments workload, another source of anxiety and tension. Every manager recognises that work demands promote anxiety but few realise that it is not confined to just the employees who work extended hours.

According to research, when employees decide to work extended hours, their colleagues also become increasingly anxious (Thompson, Beauvais, & Lyness, 1999). Suddenly, these colleagues become more aware of both the conflict between work and family life, as well as the benefits they could accrue from extended work hours. These colleagues then feel the strain of their family demands.

However, anxiety reflects perceived, not actual, workload. Indeed, perceived and actual workload do not always correspond. For instance, time spent on familiar and engrossing activities seems to pass quickly, whereas unfamiliar and monotonous tasks seem to span a prolonged duration — especially in the afternoon (Aschoff, 1998).

Employees should thus confine unfamiliar tasks to the morning and also limit the number of unfamiliar or monotonous tasks they complete. As a consequence, employees will perceive their workload as restricted, not extensive and work demands as reasonable, rather than excessive. Their anxiety will dissipate and their concentration will recover.

Each month or so, employees should construct a list of problems they would like to resolve. Examples might include conflicts with a friend or family member, financial difficulties, health issues, work problems or even moral dilemmas. They should identify a problem they could potentially resolve if they could uncover a suitable solution. They should then write a sentence that describes their desire to uncover a solution, such as 'Help me resolve this conflict with Bob'. Finally, they should repeat this sentence continuously for several minutes before they retire to bed.

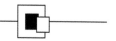

Bonuses and promotions should primarily depend upon the extent to which employees develop their skills and improve their performance.

To promote efficiency and productivity, as well as other desirable qualities, pictures of individuals who appear to demonstrate these attributes should be sought. For example, managers could attempt to locate pictures of motivated, determined, but unfamiliar individuals — such as unknown athletes. Pictures of strangers that portray only desirable qualities should be displayed in the workplace. Pictures of renowned individuals who portray undesirable qualities could also be displayed.

Finally, to ensure that individuals do not endeavour to outperform one another, bonuses, promotion or recognition should not depend on which employees were the most productive or effective. Instead, these benefits should depend on the extent to which employees demonstrated improvements in their performance or behaviour. Only employees who develop additional skills, address previous limitations and augment their productivity should be rewarded. These employees will strive to outperform themselves and not other individuals.

Chapter 4

Individual Performance

Granting Employees Autonomy

The previous chapter revealed that performance deteriorates when employees experience anxiety, unease and uncertainty. Anxiety dissipates when individuals do not feel compelled to compete with one another. Unease and uncertainty abate if employees are empowered to emphasise quality over efficiency or vice versa. Finally, tension is alleviated when workload is perceived to diminish. However, none of these practices or attributes will overcome anxiety or foster composure if individuals feel constrained, trapped or controlled. Anxiety will diminish only when managers can furnish employees with the necessary autonomy and freedom.

Employees like to feel they can decide which tasks to undertake and to determine the order in which to perform these activities. They like to feel they can select the methods they will use to complete these tasks and can decide when they will work. They like to feel autonomous, independent and liberated. They do not actually need to reach these decisions alone; but they need to feel they can.

Managers generally recognise that most employees covet and seek autonomy. Most managers, however, restrict their employees' autonomy and do not grant them the opportunity to apply their own methods and strategies. Instead, managers may stipulate the techniques that employees should utilise, as well as specifying which clients to pursue or the ways things should be done.

Few managers, however, recognise the sequence of problems that arise when autonomy is restricted. Employees who are granted autonomy — who experience a sense of control — are less likely to engage in acts that damage the organisation. According to the research, they are less inclined to squander resources, behave dishonestly, curb their effort, violate regulations or engage in theft (e.g., Boone et al., 2002). They cooperate with colleagues and assist their subordinates.

In contrast, employees who receive no autonomy, and who do not experience a sense of control, seldom assume responsibility. They blame other individuals, events and factors when shortfalls arise and may engage in deceptive, unethical acts. They are less likely to comply with expectations regarding resources, workplace behaviour or compliance with workplace policies. Indeed, studies reveal they are more likely to perpetrate hazardous, risky behaviours.

These propositions were first highlighted in a set of studies by Reiss and Mitra (1998) in which participants completed two surveys. The first was designed to highlight the mortality of participants, with questions such as 'How often do you think about how short life really is?' This survey mirrors the impact of commercials designed to promote road safety by depicting shocking accidents. The second survey ascertained the likelihood that participants would engage in particular risks.

Relative to other individuals, participants who seldom feel a sense of control — who seldom feel impervious to factors they cannot control — were more likely to engage in risks after they considered their mortality. In other words, these individuals are more likely to drive precariously after they observe campaigns that are intended to promote road safety — a shocking discovery.

Research indicates many other positive outcomes fostered by autonomy (Rogelberg, Barnes-Farrell, & Creamer, 1999). Employees who are granted autonomy do not feel constrained to pursue only the tasks they are assigned. They feel an obligation, even a motivation, to assist their colleagues. Through this process they begin to develop empathy, understanding and insight into the needs, concerns and perspectives of other individuals. This empathy further promotes their urge to support colleagues as well as friends and suppliers.

Customer service also improves markedly in response to autonomy. When granted autonomy, employees do not feel obliged to rigorously comply with company policies, standards, customs and procedures. They can therefore adapt their behaviour to fulfil the demands of clients and to accommodate the unique needs of each customer. They can be flexible and supportive, rather than rigid and unhelpful.

Despite these research findings, managers like to set specific instructions and to offer specific guidelines. They like to stipulate the methods that employees should apply to complete their tasks. Unfortunately, many of these instructions, guidelines and methods actually compromise performance.

For example, managers often encourage their employees to appear cheerful and relaxed when they interact with customers, suppliers and even colleagues. They advocate that employees should seem content and composed even if they feel frustrated, uneasy, or anxious. Yet, scholars have unearthed some of the unfortunate and neglected consequences of these practices. Employees who pretend to feel cheerful or relaxed — who feign enthusiasm and composure — are less likely to be perceived by their customers as friendly, warm and polite. By exhibiting smiles that are not authentic, that involve the contraction of a unique set of facial muscles, customers will perceive them as deceptive rather than genuine, as manipulative rather than cooperative.

In addition, the employees merely experience additional stress and tension from this discrepancy between the emotions they display and the emotions they feel. Ultimately, this discrepancy induces a sense of exhaustion and dissatisfaction.

By contrast, some managers grant considerable autonomy to their employees. They allow employees to utilise any methods, techniques, approaches and tactics they believe are suitable. But, this autonomy can also present some unintended complications (see also MacKenzie, Podsakoff, & Ahearne, 1998). When autonomy is granted, employees may feel a sense of uncertainty, a sense of trepidation. This uncertainty can sometimes impede their motivation and focus, causing them to adjust their goals or switch sporadically between activities. Their performance may deteriorate, as does their confidence. They approach each task with a sense of apprehension rather than enthusiasm, enjoying few activities and experiencing resentment towards their job, manager, peers and organisation. Thus, autonomy can sometimes actually impair motivation.

To override this apprehension — to forge a sense of certainty — managers may offer additional support and guidance and provide more advice and feedback. Yet, according to some vital but unanticipated scientific findings, even this provision of feedback can promote job dissatisfaction (Singh, 1998). Managers who provide feedback too often will tend to intrude upon employees' autonomy. They may restrict the employees' sense of control, responsibility and confidence. Indeed, scientists have demonstrated that extensive feedback — coupled with considerable autonomy — tends to induce dissatisfaction, frustration and even resentment.

In 1998, Jagdip Singh undertook research to examine whether or not managers who often provide feedback and guidance tend to influence the attitudes of sales employees. Specifically, the extent to which these sales employees receive feedback, experience tension and feel their role is clear and specific was surveyed.

Employees who received clear, specific roles were less likely to experience tension at work if their managers often provided feedback. In contrast, employees who received autonomous roles were more likely to experience tension at work if their managers often, compared to seldom, provided feedback. Advice and guidance actually promoted stress in these employees. Presumably, the managers' feedback somehow conflicts with the goals and objectives that employees set themselves.

To foster an appropriate level of autonomy, employees should be asked to plan the goals they will pursue, the targets they will achieve and the methods they will utilise. They should then be able to specify when they would like to receive approval, guidance and feedback from managers.

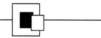

Employees should be encouraged to confront anxiety, frustration, or other unpleasant emotions. They should focus upon these emotional obstacles and defer other activities. When autonomy is granted, extensive feedback can be counterproductive.

Employees who interact with customers should not be encouraged to pretend to be cheerful or relaxed when they actually feel frustrated or anxious. Instead, whenever they experience unpleasant emotions, they should first concede some of their feelings, such as, 'That makes me feel a bit upset'. They should then attempt to suspend the discussion, perhaps using a statement such as, 'I hadn't considered that. Just give me a second to explore that further'. They could relocate to a private room or some other location for a minute or so.

Another strategy may be to form an image of an acquaintance they do not respect who often seems uneasy, restless and troubled. These images tend to alleviate unpleasant emotions, because individuals feel calm and composed by comparison (e.g., Haddock, Macrae, & Fleck, 2002).

Driving Innovation and Creativity

In a nutshell, autonomy alleviates anxiety, promotes ethics, minimises risks, fosters cooperation and improves customer service — provided that employees create unequivocal roles themselves and that managers do not convey too much advice or feedback. Autonomy also stimulates one more benefit, perhaps the most vital determinant of workplace performance — innovation.

When autonomy is restricted, creativity tends to be stifled. Managers who impose specific tasks, restrictions and criteria can create an enviroment where employees feel inhibited to explore novel solutions and approaches. When workplace problems and issues are not resolved creatively or effectively, products and services tend to be banal and trite, rather than innovative and insightful. Improvements to workplace strategies and operations are limited, as narrow rules do not promote open minds. A plethora of studies have revealed that autonomy fosters creativity, innovation, initiative and insight (see George & Zhou, 2001).

Nevertheless, autonomy is not the only key to creativity. Many other factors need to be considered. For instance, many recruiters strive to select the most creative, innovative or original applicants. Yet they may be unable to differentiate creative applicants from other candidates; most recruiters select the applicants who seem intelligent, articulate and informed.

Scientific evidence, however, does not align with this tendency to select the most prized, diligent and intelligent. Creative individuals are not always (and indeed are seldom) the most intelligent, articulate, informed or even productive employees. For example, individuals who prefer to work methodically, systematically and carefully — a profile many managers seek and admire — seldom engender creative, innovative solutions (Fritzsche, McIntire, & Yost, 2002). Their disciplined, formal inclination tends to stifle creative thoughts and insights.

Recruiters also prefer employees who were raised in stable, solid families and may exclude employees who may appear confronting or more aggressive. Yet, Koestner, Walker and Fichman (1999) revealed these employees tend to be more creative and innovative, more original and insightful. Employees who had experienced many disputes in their family environment learn to reconcile conflicting opinions and strive to accommodate contradictory perspectives. These experiences promote an original, novel, unique and complex outlook that ultimately enhances their creative skills and capacities.

Recruiters also tend to prefer employees who have developed extensive expertise in one discipline — such as engineering, finance, marketing, law or psychology. Research suggests this preference towards specialists undermines innovation as these individuals tend to be less creative (Geletkanycz & Black, 2001). When individuals develop an expertise in one field only, their thought processes become more efficient, streamlined and thus selective. They learn to disregard factors and considerations that are seldom consequential. By spontaneously omitting so much information, their flexibility declines and their suggestions tend to be conventional, not revolutionary; rigid, not adaptive.

In a study conducted by Geletkanycz and Black (2001), managers were asked whether they believed their organisation should adapt or maintain its strategies and practices over the next few years. Managers who had developed extensive expertise in one field usually opted to maintain the status quo. By contrast, managers who had developed modest expertise in several disciplines tended to argue their organisation should challenge the current traditions and processes. These managers championed change, progress, and development — an approach demonstrated to promote creativity and innovation in employees.

Still, an exposure to many disciplines does not overcome all barriers to creativity, and there are many other impediments to innovation. For instance, most creative endeavours proceed in a team environment with employees assembled together to stimulate, to brainstorm and to canvass ideas. Unfortunately, as suggested by several remarkable findings, these environments tend to stifle innovation (Pluatania & Moran, 2001). In team settings, individuals tend to resort to suggestions and thoughts they have entertained before — familiar ideas and concepts. Even when someone else is merely standing in the same room, occupied with his or her own thoughts, employees are less likely to explore novel ideas and to subdue their innate tendencies and habits.

For example, teachers are more likely to assign the same grade to a series of exam papers if someone else is nearby (Pluatania & Moran, 2001). Almost all of their students might receive a B grade or the same comment. The teachers tend to resort to the grade or evaluation with which they are most familiar or comfortable.

Furthermore, in team settings, individuals feel their credibility might be compromised if they propose an argument that diverges from the opinions and viewpoints of other members. They feel their reputation will dissolve if they express an opinion that challenges the prevailing stance of their team — and they are right. Scientists have revealed the credibility of individuals tends to deteriorate, not improve, when they express a unique, innovative argument (Wittenbaum, Hubbell, & Zuckerman, 1999).

To overcome these limitations, many team meetings are structured carefully and organised formally, often involving strict agendas, itineraries, lists and rules. Some of these teams might promote creative, innovative suggestions every day — unfortunately, they are usually the same creative, innovative suggestions each day.

Creativity is shown to be smothered rather than expedited by structured, formal meetings. According to recent studies, in this type of environment individuals feel they cannot stray from the issue under consideration (Okhuysen, 2001). They do not feel licensed to challenge the current practices or empowered to exhibit flexibility, initiative and innovation.

To escape the rigidity that coincides with expertise, several measures should be considered. First, some employees with only modest experience in a particular field should be invited to meetings and debates. They should be asked to contribute and offer suggestions in relation to the field in which their expertise is limited. Their suggestions will often seem uninformed and perhaps their insights appear misguided or their recommendations flawed. However, when experts attempt to counter these suggestions, to demonstrate their simplicity, their perspective improves and their biases diminish — innovative insights can emerge.

Managers and employees should receive some training in numerous disciplines, even if they are unlikely to be assigned tasks where these skills are necessary. They should develop taxation and accounting skills, be exposed to social psychology and learn to understand the technology that underpins production. This exposure conquers their tendency to disregard various factors and considerations.

This exposure also thwarts many other mental processes that stifle creativity. When employees strive for original ideas, their thoughts often become fixated upon their previous suggestion. They cannot escape from their first solution or override their original position. An exposure to a variety of topics and perspectives tends to overcome this obstruction.

Managers should also collect interesting facts in relation to their industry as well as the sectors with which they interact. They should explore their competitors' initiatives, understand and record economic trends and gather relevant scientific findings from journals. This database of facts presents two benefits. These observations provide employees with information they could broach during sales meetings and conferences to enhance their credibility. More importantly, these employees can also read this database before seeking solutions to problems or engaging in other creative activities. Such diverse concepts tend to promote innovative thought (Clapham, 2001) and to preclude rigidity. Thus, the same program can both enhance the social skills of employees as well as promote innovation.

The images that employees form in their mind, the thoughts they entertain, can also facilitate creativity. For example, employees should be encouraged to specify the various groups to which they belong — such as female, engineer and Asian. They should then identify the favourable stereotypes of these groups — such as the perception that engineers are intelligent.

These thoughts promote creativity, encourage insight and foster innovation.

Specifically, after individuals consider the favourable stereotypes of their group, they do not feel the need to overcome their shortfalls, address their deficiencies, minimise errors or work cautiously (Seibt & Forster, 2004). They become more willing to accept and embrace risks, which fosters novel, original, creative suggestions.

During the year, managers should occasionally convene unstructured meetings where unplanned issues and suggestions are explored and agendas are disregarded. Some social discussion should also be encouraged, rather than prohibited.

The physical environment can also inhibit or promote innovation. Red rather than blue surroundings have been shown to facilitate creative solutions (Soldat, Sinclair, & Mark, 1997). Throughout history, red has been connected to excitement and contentment, whereas blue has been linked to sadness and dissatisfaction. Red induces unconscious feelings of enthusiasm and contentment. When individuals are excited and content, they do not feel threatened or vulnerable but rather free to explore and acquire additional skills and insights. The unconscious experience of contentment that coincides with red surroundings has been demonstrated to promote creative, innovative thoughts. Indeed, any signals and cues in the environment that promote this contentment will usually enhance creativity.

In 2002, Ronald Friedman and Jens Forster published a remarkable discovery in the field of creativity. Participants each received a series of word puzzles. Some participants were instructed to press their palms against the bottom of a table in an upwards direction while they complete these tasks. Other participants were instructed to press their palms against the top of a table in a downwards direction. The participants performed significantly more proficiently on these tasks if they pressed their palms in an upwards direction. The researchers' interpretation of this result was that, throughout evolution, individuals tend to press their palms downwards and away from their bodies to repel some object, predator or rival. Hence, this movement is usually linked to dissatisfaction, which thus hinders creativity.

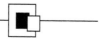

To boost innovation, employees should learn a series of techniques that foster creativity, such as reading a series of unrelated facts, recounting their strengths, and incorporating terms such as 'absorbed', 'interested', 'delighted', or 'challenge' in their solutions to workplace issues. Informal occasions are more likely to foster creativity than are formal meetings.

Finally, to enhance creativity even further, employees should be encouraged to ensure that an inspiring word — such as 'absorbed', 'interested', 'delighted', 'initiative', 'unique', or 'challenge' — is somehow included in their suggestion. They might be encouraged to develop a marketing slogan that utilises the word 'fascinate' or to construct a proposal that includes the term 'absorbed' on five occasions.

This instruction promotes a form of motivation that enhances creativity. Employees who read inspiring words such as absorbed, interested, delighted and challenge, attend to their personal interests and fascinations and become absorbed in these activities. When engrossed in the tasks they are assigned, creativity and innovation are enhanced. By contrast, employees who read words that imply obligation such as 'forced', 'pressured' and 'controlled' try to fulfil other individuals' needs. They feel less engrossed, less absorbed and their creativity wanes and originality dissipates.

Engendering Altruism

Many measures can be undertaken to foster creativity and innovation but profit may not be increased. Creativity and innovation will not always attract customers nor curb expenses. Indeed, innovation might actually damage performance if employees merely strive to improve their own status. Employees might formulate creative means to reduce their workload, appropriate funds, secure a promotion and so forth. Thus, innovation must be integrated with altruism.

Altruism is far from universal. In one financial institution, for example, employees were asked whether or not they would endorse an accounting initiative that would not affect their own pay whatsoever but would benefit their organisation immensely. The majority of employees rejected this initiative.

In some workplaces, however, employees attempt to enhance the organisation even if their individual efforts are not recognised. They may conserve resources, assist beleaguered colleagues, operate efficiently, work at home during the evenings, accept a wage reduction and comply with all regulations. Not all workplaces mirror this ideal. Yet few workplaces have instituted the appropriate set of practices, processes and policies that engender this altruism. Many avenues can be explored to encourage altruistic, rather than egocentric, attitudes.

Unsuitable decisions foster unethical employees. Reckless employees are especially prevalent in specific industries. Employees are more likely to demonstrate altruism if they believe that such altruistic behaviour is common, rather than scarce.

To illustrate, many organisations contact an employment agency to seek temporary employees during demanding periods. The employment agency can usually access a database of individuals who could fulfil the required roles and then assigns them to the organisation. Few organisations, however, evaluate the practices of these agencies or evaluate whether these agencies exhibit support, commitment and dedication to the individuals they represent. According to recent research, this oversight could be very destructive. Temporary employees usually demonstrate more altruism in the workplace if they perceive their employment agency as supportive rather than uncooperative, as obliging rather than inconsiderate, as dedicated rather than inactive (Moorman & Harland, 2002). They extend the altruism they received from one organisation to a different workplace altogether. Because of the support they received, these employees assume — perhaps unconsciously — that such altruism is rife and is appropriate.

Regrettably, managers often institute practices and policies that evince distrust, disrespect and disdain towards their employees. They might install cameras or lock cupboards. In many call centres, every key the operators press, every comment the operators utter and every occasion the operators leave their station is recorded.

Science has contested the legitimacy of these practices. Although unintended, these practices imply that employees are not trustworthy, and assume employees are seldom altruistic and have actually been shown to provoke destructive behaviours, such as theft (Greenberg & Barling, 1999).

Finally, the messages that managers publicise to foster altruistic acts are often misguided. Many managers tend to conceal rather than highlight the inconvenience of altruistic acts. Several investigations have highlighted the flaws in this approach (see Werner, Stoll, Birch, & White, 2002). Employees are more likely to comply with a message in which they are encouraged to engage in some altruistic act — such as recycle paper or aluminium cans — if the inconvenience of this act is highlighted rather than concealed. When the message does not acknowledge the inconvenience of this act, employees unconsciously assume their needs are not understood and that their feelings are not appreciated. As a consequence, they do not perceive the message as credible; they disregard the sign and they reject the message.

To overcome these issues, managers should try to maintain security and some control, but still manifest trust. To illustrate, managers can calculate many subtle indices, or measures, that gauge the prevalence of disruptive acts — without the need to increase surveillance. For instance, managers can assess the rates of absenteeism on days that are adjacent to rest days or relative to other days. Sometimes, absenteeism is elevated on Fridays or more pronounced on Mondays. These observations tend to indicate that some employees have contrived their illnesses.

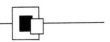

To encourage altruism, managers should demonstrate trust, admiration and empathy towards their employees. They should offer modest rewards to employees who demonstrate cooperative, supportive behaviour. Unlike sizeable incentives, modest rewards, if not distributed too frequently, do not create cynicism.

Managers can also assess whether or not telephone use is constant across the day. Sometimes, telephone use is more frequent late in the day or especially pronounced on Friday afternoon. An increased use late in the day may indicate that employees lack dedication, commitment, inspiration or focus. Finally, managers can assess stock inventories. If stock is often consumed more rapidly on days when the supervisor is absent, managers can infer the possibility of theft.

Second, for each measure, managers should determine the maximum possible level of duplicity to determine the worst scenario. Perhaps all instances of absenteeism adjoin rest days, or all telephone calls are confined to the afternoon. Perhaps all resources are stolen. Managers should then deduct the observed measure from this maximum. This value indicates the extent to which employees abstained from some disruptive act such as absenteeism/excessive phone calls/theft. This value should be publicised, as a form of praise or recognition (see Gellatly & Luchak, 1998).

Third, if the prevalence of some disruptive act rises — if the rate of absenteeism or the incidence of theft increases — some form of restriction or surveillance should be imposed without delay. Managers could demand certificates from doctors, monitor telephone calls and lock cupboards but should publicise this restriction as a temporary solution, an inescapable necessity or an unfortunate course of action. They should foster anger — controlled anger — against the perpetrators.

Fourth, employees need to be encouraged to engage in altruism, not through vacuous promises, but through genuine rewards. Employees should retain a journal that records instances in which they support colleagues, share knowledge, resolve conflicts, provide assistance, accept difficult decisions and respond appropriately to criticism. Occasionally, managers could institute some process, such as peer reviews, to ensure these journals are accurate.

These journals should be consulted during decisions that revolve around promotions or bonuses. Perhaps a minor reward, such as a gift voucher, could be presented to the employee who demonstrates the most support each month. Furthermore, managers should submit anecdotes that depict ethical, honest acts to company memoranda.

Managers may assume that such trivial rewards are futile, ineffective and even patronising. But, research has revealed that trivial incentives, even rewards the individual is likely to immediately discard, actually encourage altruism (Holmes, Miller, & Lerner, 2002). Token incentives can promote charitable behaviour. Today, most individuals actually feel a sense of shame when they exhibit altruism. They feel a sense of guilt when they sacrifice their own gains to support another individual. They are bombarded with exhortations and admonitions to be egocentric through comments such as 'Look out for number one'. So, a trivial reward or incentive that recognises their altruism overcomes this guilt or shame, and employees become more likely to demonstrate cooperation and support.

Signs and messages that are intended to promote some altruistic act, such as recycling, should acknowledge the inconvenience or distress. They could utilise phrases such as 'We know it's inconvenient, but it's vital for the company' or 'We know you're busy, but we would really appreciate your assistance'. These signs should also utilise the terms 'we' or 'our', rather than 'I' or 'my', as the former promote cooperation not competition — as demonstrated by a diverse range of studies (e.g., Fitzsimons & Kay, 2004).

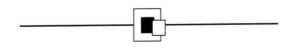

Chapter 5

Addressing Undesirable Behaviour

Rejecting Suggestions

An appropriate blend of autonomy, unstructured meetings, discretionary support and rewards will promote innovative, altruistic suggestions and proposals. Yet, managers will not always utilise these suggestions. Even the most intelligent managers may sometimes reject suggestions that could have advanced the organisation, or dismiss solutions that could have resolved recurring problems.

Indeed, scientific studies suggest the most novel, original or revolutionary proposals are also the most likely to be rejected (Ford & Gioia, 2000).

Managers need to consider a variety of factors when they evaluate suggestions, for example market trends, rival merchandise, processing costs, appearance and many other issues. Yet, they cannot possibly consider every one of these factors. So, instead, they develop simple criteria to evaluate suggestions. They might accept only the products that resemble previous successes or only accept the solutions that involve few individuals. Novel suggestions, however, depart from previous concepts and thus seldom fulfil these simple criteria — original solutions are often discarded prematurely.

Even managers who consider every suggestion carefully, or who evaluate every decision methodically, can demonstrate some striking flaws. To illustrate one of these flaws, consider managers who have invested an enormous sum of money into some computer software, a package that is plagued with errors and problems. Now, suppose an employee proposes to create a rival, improved package at virtually no cost. Some managers would reject the improved package. 'But, we have devoted so much money to the other software' or 'we would be wasting our investment', they would assert.

They would be unaware of the remarkable fallacy they have committed. They would not recognise that the previous investment is entirely immaterial or that these expenses have already been paid. They should select the option that would reap the most benefits in the future, but instead, they retain the course of action in which they have invested their resources and effort. Recruiters strive to attract managers who are not susceptible to these biases and flaws. They strive to attract managers who have succeeded, thrived and prevailed in the past.

Astonishingly and perhaps paradoxically, scientists have discovered that individuals who have demonstrated previous success are more likely to exhibit these biases (e.g., Bragger, 2003). Managers who have been successful are particularly likely to reject suggestions or initiatives that depart from the practices they instituted. They ascribe their success to the practices they implemented, the principles they followed and the skills they utilised — assuming that novel concepts are ineffective or inappropriate. Research reveals that managers who perceive themselves as successful are more likely to reach flawed decisions regarding their purchases or investments in the future.

Likewise, organisations perceived as leaders in their field are also more likely to reach inappropriate decisions. For example, they are more likely to purchase the latest technology, regardless of its applicability, merely to maintain their reputation (Flanagin, 2000).

Some managers strive to circumvent these biases or distortions. They consider every decision or issue carefully and systematically, so their decisions become less susceptible to superficial, extraneous factors. Their decisions become less dependent upon the appearance of some individual or document — their decisions become less dictated by their reputation.

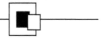

Employer suggestions that seem implausible should be retained in a database, together with the conditions or occasions in which these initiatives might be more viable.

But this systematic approach does not enable them to consider a multitude of issues simultaneously or to balance conflicting needs. Indeed, studies reveal that individuals who always consider issues methodically or compare options systematically often do not reach appropriate decisions. When each alternative course of action presents many benefits, drawbacks or unpredictable outcomes, these managers seldom reach the optimal decision (Riding & Wigley, 1997).

Thus, managers should never reject creative ideas nor criticise or discard novel solutions but should store all innovative suggestions. In addition, they should identify instances in which these innovations could be beneficial — perhaps once the market declines, or the dollar improves. These conditions should be stored together with each suggestion; then, as soon as these conditions arise, the suggestions should be reconsidered.

The Need for Self-Awareness

When managers evaluate suggestions, proposals and initiatives, their own biases, insecurities and tendencies tend to obscure their evaluations. Somehow managers need to address these biases and to accommodate these shortfalls. Unfortunately, many factors can obstruct this endeavour or perpetuate, rather than eradicate, these biases. However, all of these factors can be tempered if managers recognise their deficits; if managers fulfil one goal — self-awareness.

Few managers are aware of all their limitations and deficiencies. One corporate insider story features an executive who requested a new laptop computer but, several days later, complained it was defective. The IT department determined that the computer was in fact sound and it was the executive who did not know how to operate it properly. The IT people thus changed the logo displayed when the computer was activated, attached some instructions and then returned the laptop — which they claimed was an updated model. The executive never complained again.

Many of the problems that haunt organisations can be ascribed to this limited awareness. Studies reveal that managers who overestimate their skills and talents tend to be liked by authorities, but not subordinates. Managers who receive the confidence and respect of their superiors — but not their subordinates — usually ascend the corporate ladder rapidly. They are often perceived as firm, uncompromising and effective. Yet managers who are admired only by their superiors can cripple workplace performance (Sosik & Megerian, 1999). They have been shown to disregard their faults, deficiencies and limitations, primarily to maintain their pride and confidence.

The result is that these managers quash any initiative that could threaten their image or endanger their dignity and status. As a consequence, they suppress the development of their subordinates; subsequently innovation diminishes and performance deteriorates.

Managers who overestimate their talents and contribution also impair many other facets of the work milieu, according to a broad range of studies (Fox & Weber, 2002). For example, managers who feel unduly confident in their decisions and policies are more likely to engage in unnecessary risks — misguided investments, unsafe practices or unusual products. Furthermore, some managers believe they can plan, schedule, monitor and refine the activities of their workgroup more effectively than can other individuals. According to subordinates, these same managers are usually less able to foster motivation, to promote communication or to encourage skill development in their team.

In one comprehensive study, managers completed two surveys. The first survey examined the extent to which these managers believed they could plan, schedule, monitor and refine the activities of their workgroup effectively. The second survey examined the extent to which these managers believed they could foster motivation, communication and skill development in their workgroup. In addition, subordinates evaluated these managers on the same behaviours. Managers who believed their ability to plan, schedule, monitor and refine activities was advanced were more likely to assert their ability to foster motivation, communication and skill development was also elevated. Conversely, the same managers were more likely to be perceived by subordinates as incompetent on these facets of behaviour (Shipper & Davy, 2002).

Managers who inflate their own skills or contributions do not only undermine their workgroup but also compromise their own development, performance and satisfaction. For example, managers who overestimate their skills — and thus disavow their limitations — have been shown to be less proficient, informed or skilled (Martacchio & Judge, 1997). They fail to recognise the need to address their deficiencies and hence seldom engage in activities that advance their expertise.

This ignorance does not promote universal bliss. Individuals who overestimate their ability often set lofty goals, elevated targets and challenging objectives. But, they seldom realise these aspirations and may experience a sense of failure, defeat and disappointment (Hurley, 1997). They will tend to ascribe these failures to factors they could not control — faulty equipment, misleading instructions and incompetent colleagues. Yet, despite their ability to explicate these failures, they feel frustration and resentment.

Sadly, these managers are not aware of their inclination to overestimate their talents. Nobody highlights their delusions nor alludes to their misconceptions; instead they tend to receive praise and admiration. According to recent research, employees try to ingratiate themselves to managers they perceive as neither supportive nor understanding (Shore, Adams, & Tashchian, 1998). They attempt to attract, please and inveigle these managers and to derive the support and cooperation they seldom receive — and so, the oblivion of these managers continues.

Indeed, managers who do not reflect upon their limitations, deliberate over their errors or regret their blunders are sometimes esteemed and honoured. Senior managers often proclaim that regret is unnecessary and management consultants have been known to state that regret is debilitating.

The scientific community, however, has highlighted the folly of this assumption. Employees who regret previous actions, reflect upon previous blunders and consider previous failures tend to reach decisions more effectively and behave more appropriately (Kray & Galinsky, 2003). These employees often consider the outcomes that would have arisen — the triumphs they would have achieved, the difficulties they would have encountered — had they acted differently. Their ability to predict consequences and complications improves. With minimal effort, they foresee the benefits, drawbacks, obstacles and intricacies of each decision. As a consequence, they tend to consider decisions more carefully and reach decisions more appropriately.

Promoting Self-Awareness

To promote employee self-awareness, managers might implement a survey in which employees rate the workplace, not their supervisor, on a set of concrete attributes. Examples could include 'In my workgroup, suggestions from employees are often implemented' or 'The tasks that I perform utilise many of my skills, talents and knowledge'. Second, managers of each workgroup should not receive the precise ratings of their employees. Instead, they should be told the extent to which previous concerns in their workgroup had been addressed, as well as the extent to which their own assessments align with their subordinates.

Managers who receive unfavourable outcomes on these indices — and thus show they have not redressed past shortfalls, not aligned with the viewpoint of their employees or not advanced the work environment — should receive no reward. They should be penalised, perhaps through a diminution of their responsibility.

These procedures can be illuminating, effective and consequential. Employees are more likely to be honest if the questions are not directed towards a particular individual. Employees are more likely to be honest if their precise responses are confidential. Managers have been shown to respond actively when they recognise that responses are honest rather than manipulative (Funderburg & Levy, 1997). They adapt their behaviour when they recognise the feedback is sincere not duplicitous.

The extent to which self-evaluations of managers align with the perceptions of their employees should be measured each year. Self-awareness develops when managers recognise they could be disadvantaged if their evaluations do not align with the perceptions of their subordinates. These procedures, however, need to be implemented with diplomacy and dignity.

Dealing With Prejudice

Promoting self-awareness in managers and employees will not however eradicate all inflated self-opinions, as some biases and distortions will persist. Perhaps the most menacing of these biases is the racism and prejudice to which all people are susceptible.

Individuals in the workplace tend to evaluate the same act more favourably if perpetrated by a member of their own group. Every individual is more prejudiced and biased than perhaps they recognise.

Most employees prefer workgroups in which the members are homogenous and uniform; they may prefer a workgroup in which everyone is young or female or an engineer for example. As a consequence, managers strive to form workgroups in which the individuals are similar and compatible.

Unfortunately, this practice conflicts with scientific discoveries that show diverse workgroups offer a broader range of perspectives and thus are more creative, more innovative and more insightful (Chatman & Flynn, 2001; Swann Jr, Kwan, Polzer, & Milton, 2003). They are oblivious to the finding that diverse workgroups are more likely to be sensitive to the unique needs and concerns of each individual. Scientific findings show that all the initial concerns, discomfort and distrust that diversity can provoke tend to evaporate within a few weeks.

These prejudices, although inevitable and ubiquitous, are especially intense in some employees. In particular, some employees believe that everyone should comply with the rules, values and customs that authorities set; that everyone should conform to tradition. Indeed, managers are more likely to respect — and indeed more likely to promote — employees who embrace the practices, traditions and customs of the organisation.

Research suggests this respect is unfounded (Reynolds, Turner, Haslam, & Ryan, 2001). Employees who perceive the values and customs of the organisation as appropriate, obligatory and virtuous do not accept practices that conflict with their traditions. They are thus less likely to accept other races or religions and more likely to feel disdain towards other ethnicities and beliefs.

In addition, many employees believe that people cannot modify their basic personality and characteristics. The attributes, deficiencies, tendencies of individuals are perceived as fixed and permanent. Individuals who are incompetent will always remain incompetent; those who are shifty will always remain shifty.

The risks of this attitude are that the beliefs of these individuals also do not change (Plaks, Stroessner, Dweck, & Sherman, 2001). They regard information that conflicts with their beliefs as anomalous, irreconcilable or inconsequential. They disregard conflicting material and thus their stereotypes persist and their misconceptions linger.

Of course, many organisations have introduced programs to curb racism, sexism, ageism and any other form of prejudice they can identify. In these programs, instructors strive passionately to demonstrate that prejudice is immoral, unfair, unenlightened and unacceptable.

Yet, most of these programs fail to purge the implicit, latent prejudices and biases that contaminate the thoughts and actions of too many employees. The behaviours of these employees might change, their assertions might evolve, but their attitudes remain intact. Although sometimes unaware of these attitudes, their prejudices and biases persist. Indeed, their prejudices and biases may deepen and intensify.

For example, the instructors of these programs will often illustrate the astounding contributions of various minorities, outlining remarkable discoveries and scholastic achievements of particular individuals.

But, according to some edifying studies, these anecdotes have been shown to exacerbate, not improve, the resentment and antipathy that employees feel (Ho, Sanbonmatsu, & Aikimoto, 2002). The reasoning is that disadvantaged individuals who are industrious and responsible can fulfil their goals; disadvantaged individuals who are intelligent and insightful can advance their standing in society; and disadvantaged individuals who are disciplined and dedicated can surmount their predicaments. Employees may incorrectly assume from these examples that deprived communities that have not been able to attain this success or to raise their status, must not be sufficiently industrious, responsible, insightful, intelligent or disciplined. Their disdain grows.

In contrast, some instructors emphasise the deprivation, hardship and abject poverty of specific communities. They might relate the injustices and misfortunes that indigenous individuals in Australia have endured since the introduction of European civilisation. They might detail the destitution and distress that many African Americans experience every day.

But, yet again, science has highlighted the dangers of this practice (Guimand & Dambrum, 2002). These accounts do not always nullify the prejudice that employees experience but instead may incite prejudice and provoke intolerance. In particular, employees attempt to justify that indeed their fortune is deserved, their wealth is warranted and their status is fitting. They attempt to identify the shortfalls of other races and to uncover the errors that precluded the ascendancy of other ethnicities.

To curb biases, some organisations even offer rewards and incentives to individuals, workgroups or departments that address prejudice, discrimination and harassment. Employees who introduce initiatives that promote tolerance, workgroups that recruit minorities or departments in which complaints have plummeted, receive some bonus or recognition.

However, scientists have demonstrated that such incentives actually promote prejudice (Monin & Miller, 2001) and amplify racism and sexism. The individuals, workgroups or department that receive rewards are actually more likely to demonstrate racism, intolerance and bias in the future.

To illustrate, in one laboratory experiment, participants received a job description and were asked whether or not the job was more suitable to men. Earlier, some of these participants were asked whether or not they agree or disagree with a series of sexist statements, such as 'Most women are not really smart'. Virtually, all participants disagreed with these statements. This procedure was intended to enable these participants to demonstrate they were unprejudiced and unbiased.

Participants who had completed this survey and thus demonstrated their tolerance were more likely to believe that men were more suited to the job than women (Monin & Miller, 2001). In other words, after individuals can demonstrate they are unprejudiced, they become more willing to demonstrate their innate biases. They do not feel the need to conceal these biases as they believe their image as a tolerant, unprejudiced individual will remain intact.

To ameliorate prejudice, programs that ridicule, mock and disparage racist, biased individuals tend to be effective if managers publicise the frailties, liabilities and malice that characterise prejudiced individuals (e.g., Bizman & Yinon, 2001).

For example, prejudiced employees feel anxious, apprehensive and afraid when they interact with minorities but they tend to ascribe this tension to other individuals, not their own deficiencies. Prejudiced individuals also overestimate their skills and perceive their own gender, ethnicity or discipline as superior (Rudman, Greenwald, & McGhee, 2001). In reality, their thoughts are usually rigid, inflexible and banal, rather than creative, innovative and unique. Finally, prejudiced individuals tend to perceive authorities as more superior, as more noble, than does everyone else. They strive desperately to climb the corporate ladder, to reach the echelons they admire and respect. In doing so, they become manipulate, deceitful, egocentric or ruthless.

To accommodate their anxiety, prejudiced employees should not be assigned roles that involve any interaction with clients, suppliers or even other departments. Due to their rigid thoughts, they should not be assigned to workgroups that strive to foster progress or improvement. Recognising their conceited, egocentric tendencies, they should not be granted roles that involve the assessment, development and support of other individuals. Strongly prejudiced individuals are suited to few roles.

Ridicule is not the only option to shatter prejudice. Research demonstrates that individuals overrate the diversity of their own ethnic group (Park, Wolsko, & Judd, 2001). Many individuals perceive other racial groups as uniform or homogenous. Thus, when they encounter a person that conflicts with their stereotype, their attitudes do not change. They perceive this instance as atypical, as anomalous. This resistance to changing views can dissipate when they recognise that all racial or ethnics groups comprise many distinct categories or clusters.

Managers may use an employee training forum to address this issue. Participants should be asked to depict their interactions with other racial or ethnic groups outside work. If possible, they should specify the subgroup of this race, ethnicity or religion — perhaps by indicating the particular sects of any individuals they have encountered or befriended or their language spoken.

Participants will usually — but not invariably — recount positive, pleasant, favourable experiences and anecdotes. Research reveals that prejudices begin to dissolve after employees hear their colleagues, peers or friends recount favourable incidents with minorities (Stangor, Sechrist, & Jost, 2001). Prejudiced employees may disregard strangers' input, but they will heed that of their colleagues.

Managers should be instructed to withdraw prejudiced employees from roles that involve leadership or creativity. This policy ensures the deficiencies of prejudiced employees do not undermine workplace performance, as well as instilling a sense of shame in these individuals.

Participants could be asked to identify instances in which they witness prejudice, bias or discrimination. These participants should then concede whether or not they have previously exhibited any of these acts. But, they should first be forewarned that individuals who claim to have never exhibited prejudice or to have never been biased, tend to overestimate their skills and inflate their abilities.

Dealing With Sexism

Despite these initiatives, many employees may continue to perceive their own race as superior. They might not perceive their ethnicity as particularly intelligent, disciplined, modest, understanding, athletic or attractive — but they believe they are superior nonetheless.

For example, relative to individuals from Asian descent, scientists reveal that Anglo Saxons are more likely to overestimate their skills, blame subordinates unfairly, fail to assist a colleague, as well as portray conceit and arrogance (Endo, Heine, & Lehman, 2000). Yet, they still perceive themselves as superior. Indeed, most cultures overrate the significance of their own ethnicity.

While racism and a sense of superiority is upsetting, sexism can be even more damaging. A manager at a large organisation recently asserted, 'What you see as a glass ceiling, I see as a protective barrier'.

Sexism promotes sexual harassment — offensive jokes, blackmail, unwanted sexual advances, discrimination and even assault. Individuals who are the victims of sexual harassment feel helpless and vulnerable, stressed and tense. To overcome these feelings they begin to withdraw from work and may become less reliable, punctual, cooperative or involved. This withdrawal diminishes the respect they receive from other employees, and their sense of frustration and vulnerability increases further.

Often, they do not understand their own reactions or emotions and may feel even more helpless and vulnerable — a vicious cycle can develop. As these feelings persist, the employees become frustrated that neither their colleagues nor managers can alleviate the problems, which induces more resentment, distrust and alienation. As they become increasingly helpless, they do not undertake active measures to counteract this problem; they deny their anguish to themselves and other individuals (see Schneider, Swan, & Fitzgerald, 1997).

Victims of harassment often do not receive the support they need, and their colleagues often blame them as the cause of their own predicament. Unwittingly, colleagues perceive these victims as more egocentric, unstable and naïve (Kaiser & Miller, 2001). These colleagues feel a sense of control, a sense they could protect themselves from a similar incident, whenever they blame the victim.

Some managers assume that women who occupy senior positions are not subjected to sexism. They assume that female board members, executives or strategic managers are less vulnerable to prejudice. Scientific research, lamentably, reveals that senior women are perhaps the most vulnerable to sexism (Heilman, Wallen, Fuchs, & Tamkins, 2004). In contrast to their male counterparts, successful females are often perceived to be unfriendly, insincere, hostile and assumed to be merely fortunate, especially in industries that are dominated by men.

In particular, individuals who do not comply with the stereotypes that pervade society or the expectations within the workforce, tend to be disliked and distrusted. Females are expected to be unsuccessful in male industries, such as engineering, and to occupy junior or administrative positions. Females who become successful violate these expectations and stereotypes, and thus tend to be both mistrusted and mistreated.

Employees who claim to be the victims of sexual harassment should clearly receive immediate support. Managers should ensure that extensive investigation does not delay responses; otherwise, employees do not disclose future incidents (Malamut & Offerman, 2001). In addition, to invite disclosure, managers should occasionally discuss their own lives with employees — with all employees — to forge a culture in which personal issues are discussed, where sensitive problems are disclosed.

Managers should also provide support to reduce the stress that harassed individuals endure, at both work and home. For instance, these individuals should be granted more authority and thus a sense of control over their lives. Their deadlines should be relaxed to enable them to optimise quality.

Sexist individuals should not be recruited, especially in organisations in which the majority of employees are male. During interviews, males who maintain eye contact with females inordinately, but orient their body in another direction tend to perceive women as submissive, as inferior (Murphy, Driscoll, & Kelly, 2002). These applicants should not be selected.

> *Recruiters should introduce tactics to identify sexist job applicants. Managers should concede their own personal concerns and problems to employees, partly to forge a sensitive, empathic culture.*

Some more advanced technologies have also been developed to identify individuals with sexist attitudes, even when these biases are covert or when this sexism is subtle. For example, in one technique formulated to uncover implicit sexism, a sequence of words appears on a screen. Participants are instructed to press the left of two buttons if a male name appears and the right of two buttons if a female name appears. They are also told to press one button if a word that is synonymous with power appears and the other button if a word that is synonymous with warmth and nurturing appears. Sexist participants — individuals who express adverse attitudes towards women — perform this task more effectively if the same button pertains to both males and power (Rudman, Greenwald, & McGhee, 2001).

Whenever individuals — especially females — are promoted to senior positions, they should be granted the opportunity to submit a profile of themselves to a workplace newsletter or memorandum. They should be encouraged to highlight their compassion and sincerity, perhaps also describing some of the community activities they have undertaken. They could underscore some of their limitations and concerns. These activities are intended to counter the stereotypes of successful women — to contradict the assumption that senior females are often hostile and insincere.

Undue Ambition

To reiterate, numerous defects and flaws promote prejudice and sexism: excessive social anxiety, rigidity, conceit and ambition — all of which can be addressed. All of these defects must be addressed, not only to stem intolerance but also to enhance many other facets of the workplace. For example, undue ambition — the zealous need to lead, command, dominate and authorise — provokes prejudice as well as many other undesirable outcomes.

Employees who are especially ambitious and hungry for success have been shown to be more critical and less encouraging. They attempt to assert their authority and superiority as they provide feedback and advice. They reduce confidence, motivation and satisfaction in everyone they encounter on their journey to success. For example, in a utilities company inhouse HR opinion survey, all the employees were asked to specify the principal drawback of their organisation. Over 480 of the 500 employees alluded to the CEO — an astonishing percentage — with statements such as 'He's too pigheaded and determined' or 'His ambition is pathological' (personal communication).

Some managers inadvertently cultivate ambition in their employees. They unwittingly manufacture a sense of superiority and competition. For example, employees who seem upset are often encouraged to consider and recognise the extent to which their life is better than citizens in many other nations or employees in many other organisations.

Scientists have identified some unexpected, but debilitating, problems that arise from this practice (Emmons & McCullough, 2003). When individuals reflect upon the facets of their life that are more fortunate than other individuals, they attempt to maintain this imbalance. Hence, they feel the need to compete with other individuals and thus experience the stress of competition and the anxiety of isolation. Conversely, when individuals reflect upon the facets of their life for which they are grateful and thankful, they do not attempt to maintain this imbalance. They feel supported, not obstructed, by society. They feel confident and resilient rather than competitive and isolated.

Most recruiters and managers, however, seek applicants who are driven to achieve and determined to succeed, who are eager to impress rather than complacent or gratified. Employees who do not work extended hours — who do not dedicate their life to the organisation — are perceived as neither committed nor productive. However, many studies have revealed this esteem towards ambitious employees is groundless (e.g., Tang & Ibrahim, 1998) Ambitious, determined employees do not assist individuals who cannot return this favour. They do not support and empathise with colleagues who cannot fulfil their needs. Nor do they enhance workplace performance, unless their efforts are recognised or rewarded. They may not comply with rules and policies such as safety regulations and thus might jeopardise the welfare of colleagues. They do not act ethically and honestly.

Ultimately, their distrust may permeate into every corner of the organisation. In distrusting environments, initiatives that usually enhance motivation and productivity actually damage performance. For example, meetings in which managers seek the opinions and feedback of employees tend to coincide with decrements — not improvements — in workplace performance.

This observation was discovered by two researchers, Danny Miller and Jangwoo Lee in 2001. They examined the financial performance — return on assets — of numerous companies. For each company, the extent to which employees feel a sense of trust towards the organisation was assessed, as was the degree to which managers consult employees to reach decisions.

When employees trust the organisation, discussion and consultation between managers and employees was found to increase return on assets. Conversely, when employees do not trust the organisation, these consultations did not increase, and could even decrease, return on assets. In a distrusting environment, individuals strive to exploit initiatives and programs, which undermines the effects of these programs.

Employees who are especially ambitious do not only damage the lives of other individuals; they damage their own lives as well. Studies reveal that individuals who are particularly ambitious and also perceive wealth as an important sign of success are less likely to be satisfied with their job, their colleagues or their remuneration.

The longevity of extremely ambitious individuals also tends to be curtailed. A study of US presidents, shows individuals who received this office while still quite young were more likely to die sooner. The same outcome was evident for Nobel Prize winners who received the award while still young (see McCann, 2001). These findings accord with the proposition that individuals who are unduly ambitious do not live as long as do their counterparts.

Furthermore, in many organisations, recruiters and managers prefer employees who are driven to boost their status and accumulate wealth. They assume that employees who crave prestige, who covet prosperity, will be determined, resolute, passionate and thus successful.

Several sophisticated investigations, however, suggest this assumption is unsound (e.g., Mumford, et al., 2002). When such employees undertake tasks at work — such as construct business plans, develop advertising campaigns and resolve issues — their attention is partly distracted by the rewards, recognition or respect they could secure. They are, therefore, seldom engrossed in the tasks they complete at work.

When individuals are not entirely absorbed in their work — when they are distracted by the prospect of rewards and recognition — their solutions and suggestions do not depart from traditional, conventional and thus sometimes obsolete practices. Their originality and creativity thus wane.

In contrast, research reveals that employees who value friend-ships and human rights over money or status tend to be more creative, innovative and effective than are other individuals.

Ambitious, determined employees, however, tend to behave appropriately, ethically and supportively in particular envi-ronments. For example, ambitious employees tend to be more sincere when executives denounce dishonesty in annual reports and memoranda, with statements such as 'Employees who are dishonest to customers will be penalised harshly' or 'Managers who conceal information from their employees will be reprimanded'.

Most organisations, however, do not denounce dishonesty in these publications, believing that such admonitions are futile and hollow. They might believe that such admonitions imply that many employees are dishonest or that they detract from the optimism and passion these publications are intended to incite.

Contrary to these assumptions, scientific advances have revealed that such admonitions are effective (Aquino, 1998). Some employees convince themselves that deceit is rife, inevitable or acceptable — hence, they feel no guilt or shame when they lie. But, condemnations of dishonesty demonstrate that deceit is neither inevitable nor acceptable. Accordingly, when employees contemplate deception, they feel a sense of guilt and thus an obligation to express the truth after they read these condemnations.

Somehow, managers need to curtail excessive ambition, to substitute this passion to achieve personal success with a yearning to assist others. Managers need to supplant selfish motives with ethical pursuits. Fortunately, some strategies for-mulated to foster ethics and morality are effective.

For example, workgroups should first discuss the benefits and the drawbacks of various principles — such as equality, honesty, empathy, safety or family. They should then identify measures that could be undertaken to redress these draw-backs. Few individuals can unearth more than four or five drawbacks of equality, honesty, empathy, safety and family.

But, even if these drawbacks cannot be redressed, such discussions and debates tend to promote ethical behaviour.

To demonstrate, Gregory Maio and his colleagues in 2001 undertook a study in which some of the participants were encouraged to identify both the benefits and drawbacks of equality in the workplace. The remaining participants did not engage in this discussion. Later, the extent to which the participants practised equality was evaluated. Specifically, these individuals undertook a task that ascertained whether or not they would discriminate against a member of another group.

Participants who had discussed the benefit and drawbacks of equality were less likely to discriminate unfairly. Under stress, most individuals relinquish their values, such as equality, honesty, safety and cooperation. They do not perceive these values as rational or logical and hence regard such ideals as debilitating during stressful conditions. But, when these values are discussed and debated, employees begin to recognise, or at least assume, that such ideals reflect rational and logical arguments and sound principles. Hence, individuals are less likely to relinquish values that have been debated, even if this discussion uncovers many drawbacks.

To instil a sense of confidence and enthusiasm, as well as a desire to cooperate rather than compete, employees should first be encouraged to identify two or three individuals who have offered support and assistance at some stage during their life. They might envisage a friend who offered some insightful advice or perhaps a distant relation who provided valuable resources.

They should then form an image of a scene in which they thank these individuals. Perhaps they could imagine simply buying a present or even a drink to demonstrate their appreciation. They could even undertake, rather than merely imagine, this act. They should also identify one or two attributes or qualities they share with their closest friends for which they are grateful, such as their health or social network. This exercise, which promotes life satisfaction and ethical behaviour, should be repeated regularly.

Appraisal

None of these initiatives — such as intense debates or official proclamations — will foster ethical acts unless such behaviour is appraised, recognised and rewarded. Unfortunately, managers seldom assess their subordinates appropriately. They may appraise the contributions and effort of employees inaccurately or evaluate the behaviour of their subordinates unfairly and unjustly, producing biases, even when they strive to be fair and they believe they are accurate. The criticisms, doubts and suspicions of managers often reflect their own defects (see Green & Sedikides, 2001).

For example, managers who are often dishonest are more likely to claim their subordinates are duplicitous. Managers who are idle are more likely to perceive their employees as unmotivated. Managers who are uncooperative are more likely to regard their subordinates as competitive.

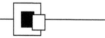

The drawbacks of various ethical values, such as cooperation and honesty, should be debated formally. Measures to address the drawbacks should be considered.

In the Green and Sedikides study, participants received an excerpt that described the behaviours, characteristics, tendencies and lifestyle of a sample individual. Some of these behaviours indicated the individual was independent and assertive — for example, this individual had travelled extensively. Other behaviours indicated the individual was dependent and submissive — for example, the individual regularly visited family.

Participants who themselves were independent and assertive were less likely to perceive this individual as dependent and submissive (Green & Sedikides, 2001). Thus, managers like to perceive their own qualities and attributes as appropriate, justifiable and thus prevalent. They are more likely to recognise both their strengths and weaknesses in other individuals.

Managers exhibit many other biases and distortions that can contaminate their evaluations of subordinates. For instance, employees who challenge workplace traditions, question established practices and dispute entrenched policies tend to receive unfavourable evaluations. These employees are less likely to receive bonuses or advancement or to be trusted, admired and recruited; yet scientific findings have revealed these same employees are more likely to enhance workplace performance and progress. They are more likely to stimulate discussions that generate innovations and initiatives.

However, one bias is even more influential and damaging than other sources of contamination. Employees whom managers like, understand or resemble are especially likely to receive favourable evaluations. The employees with whom managers have developed a familiarity or bond tend to be perceived as more effective, insightful and dedicated. The employees towards whom managers have formed affection are regarded as more proficient and appropriate. This bias is especially prevalent in managers who perceive themselves as competent, gifted and worthy, and is generally not intentional, but unconscious.

Research has now confirmed that managers will tend to trivialise the faults of employees they like or resemble (Robbins & DeNisi, 1998). Egocentric behaviours may be perceived as reflecting ambition and dedication, while risky behaviours are perceived as bold and courageous. Idle behaviour may be perceived to reflect a balanced perspective. But, they do not extend this courtesy to individuals they do not like or do not resemble. A fault in a friend is endearing; a fault in a rival is enduring.

Similarly, managers will tend to ascribe the shortfalls of employees they like to factors that could have been prevented (Antonioni & Park, 2001). When their favourite employees commit an error or breach a promise, managers will ascribe these issues to the difficulty of this task or shortcomings in the instructions. Or, perhaps the individual was fatigued after the remarkable effort and dedication they had exhibited all week. Perhaps the equipment was faulty or inappropriate. But again, this rationale is not applied to employees with whom the manager has not formed a bond or affection. This rationale engenders unfair evaluations and thus frustration, distrust and disloyalty.

Daniel Beal and his colleagues (Beal, Ruscher, & Schnake, 2001) conducted research in 2001 to demonstrate that evaluations of managers are biased towards the individuals to whom they are similar. Participants received a series of anecdotes, such as 'Keisha called her brother a rude name. She had a bit of a temper. He'd been ridiculing her'. After each anecdote, participants indicated the extent to which they would ascribe the behaviour of protagonists to their character or the situation they encountered.

If protagonists were assigned a foreign name, hostile behaviours were more likely to be ascribed to their character. For protagonists without a foreign name, hostile behaviours were more likely to be ascribed to the demands and pressures of the situation.

When managers are angry and frustrated, they are especially unforgiving (see Forgas, 1999). They are unlikely to recognise the obstacles that impaired the performance of employees they do not like. Instead, they like to feel a sense of control, a sense of power — they do not like to blame shortfalls on factors they cannot control or ascribe these errors and shortcomings to task difficulty, inadequate instructions, economic decline or executive decisions. Instead they prefer to ascribe problems to individuals, especially individuals they do not like. Again, this bias is particularly conspicuous in managers who perceive themselves as competent, proficient, talented and admired.

Obviously, the extent to which a manager likes or resembles an employee should not influence evaluations. Managers do not always like employees who are most effective or those who will enhance workplace performance. Indeed, managers will often like or dislike employees as a consequence of misconceptions and misunderstandings.

For example, anxious individuals often behave politely, sometimes too politely. When individuals are anxious, they become more aware of the problems that could arise if they behave unsuitably. They strive to behave politely and courteously but their behaviour is often perceived suspiciously, as unduly polite. Managers thus tend to dislike anxious, worried individuals — not because they are ineffective, duplicitous or destructive — but merely because these employees are tense and polite (Forgas, 1999).

To purge biased appraisals, managers should ideally ensure they have experienced or performed each task they assign their employees. Employees, however, will often be instructed to complete some activity the manager themself has never undertaken. Unfortunately, studies have revealed that managers may evaluate these employees unnecessarily harshly, which provokes resentment, dissatisfaction and turnover (Lassiter & Munhall, 2001). Managers tend to overestimate their own performance on most tasks and assume their own performance exceeds average. These managers will thus believe that employees who can match or approximate their own performance on some task must also exceed average. In other words, managers will tend to overestimate the performance of an employee who undertakes an activity they have also performed before (see Lassiter & Munhall, 2001).

To eliminate these various biases, many organisations consider only concrete, objective outcomes — sales performance, production rate and so forth. Subjective measures, such as perceived effort or cooperation, are not considered. Yet unfortunately this focus on objective outcomes has been shown to impede progress (Oliver & Anderson, 1994). An emphasis on concrete criteria builds a fixation with immediate goals rather than future objectives, such as skill acquisition or relationship development. The focus on impartial assessment undermines strategic progress.

To circumvent these biases and limitations, the behaviour of each manager — such as their leadership, support and advice — should be rated by all their subordinates and peers. Managers who receive favourable rating from some individuals, but not others, probably do not reach decisions fairly. They may not reward individuals justly or support employees equitably. These managers should be asked to justify each of their decisions to the executive board, specifying the merits and drawbacks of each decision, describing the process used to gather this information. This disciplinary action has been demonstrated to promote equity and justice.

Second, to ensure that employees do not work extended hours merely to receive favourable appraisals, managers should assess the extent to which the efficiency of their subordinates has improved. Employees should record the time spent on each activity. Using this information, managers can determine if the employees' efficiency improves over time and to compare employees who undertake similar tasks. The records can be used to identify those who work efficiently and thus deserve a promotion.

Of course, some employees could fabricate these records to expedite promotions, perhaps by claiming 30 minutes devoted to a task that actually spanned one hour, or one day to a goal that had actually necessitated a week. But, these fabrications and exaggerations can be prevented. Specifically, whenever some target is reached, employees who dedicated more time to that activity should receive greater rewards. For example, if 10% of all sales is bestowed to employees, the individuals who devoted the most time to each customer should receive the highest bonus. Individuals who underestimate the time they devote to tasks will thus receive less remuneration. Individuals who overestimate the time they devote to tasks will be perceived as inefficient.

Finally, biases towards the employees that managers like can be exploited to improve workplace performance. Whenever these employees commit some error or exhibit some deficiency, all the factors that contributed to these shortfalls should be recorded. Perhaps the room was too noisy or maybe the equipment was obsolete. Managers should then introduce measures to address these factors. In particular, they should then introduce measures to ensure these same factors do not obstruct the employees with whom they have not formed an affectionate bond. This process exploits the innate tendency of managers to identify the barriers that obstructed the employees they like and to then address these obstacles to advance the performance of all individuals.

Managers who receive conflicting evaluations from their subordinates and peers should be wary of the extent to which their judgments are influenced by personal preferences. Ideally, these managers should not assess employees in the future, until their biases have been rectified.

Recognition and Rewards

Clearly, appraisals need to be integrated with an appropriate system of recognition, rewards, bonuses and incentives. Unfortunately, many systems of reward are not appropriate and foster frustration, not motivation, and resentment rather than cohesion.

To illustrate, the bonuses that teams receive often depend on concrete outcomes. Only teams with an escalating profit or elevated sales might be rewarded. Some noteworthy scientific projects have invalidated these systems (e.g., Sarin & Mahajan, 2001). These bonuses can promote motivation, but only when individuals feel they can achieve their outcome and that other factors will not impede their performance.

If the industry is particularly competitive, employees recognise that unpredictable events in the market, those they cannot prevent or control, could impede their success. They cannot dictate their performance or guarantee their own success. So, their motivation wanes and their performance deteriorates whenever their bonuses depend on concrete outcomes.

Bonuses may also engender some resentment or distress. Numerous employees overestimate their skills or overestimate their effort and contributions. They may feel they deserve more recognition than most of their colleagues. On average, of course, they receive the same recognition, rewards and bonuses as their colleagues and are less than pleased.

Indeed, employees who receive significant rewards and bonuses tend to be perceived as manipulative, deceitful or ego-centric. For instance, executives who receive appreciable benefits and incentives are sometimes regarded as shifty or selfish. However, many individuals assert that business performance will not improve until executive salaries and rewards are augmented. Executives who receive generous salaries and bonus schemes are perceived as potent and proficient.

The truth, according to science, diverges dramatically from this popular conviction (Miller & Wiseman, 2001). Employees perceive executives who receive exorbitant rewards to be uncommitted to the organisation. They are not perceived as prestigious, gifted or effective.

In 2001, Janice Miller and Robert Wiseman undertook a provocative study to examine the impact of executive salaries on reputation. Participants received a description of 16 hypothetical Chief Executive Officers (CEOs). Participants were then asked to rate the extent to which they perceive each CEO as effective, proficient and suitable. CEOs who earned an exorbitant salary were perceived as less effective in their role and concerned with their own remuneration and not the success of their company.

A variety of factors, therefore, need to be considered to ensure the system of rewards and recognition is just and effective. First, when employees do not feel they can control the outcome of their efforts, they prefer that rewards depend on the performance of the workgroup. They prefer to receive bonuses if they operate, cooperate, debate, challenge, coordinate and communicate appropriately; or if they develop additional skills, strategies and insights.

The tendency of employees to overestimate their own contributions can also be addressed, or at least moderated. Soon after the bonuses are distributed, managers should convene a meeting with their workgroup. During this meeting, every employee should attempt to identify the obstacles that limited the performance of each individual colleague.

Employees should then suggest some measure or behaviour they will undertake to preclude these obstacles in the future. They might present more comprehensive instructions to one colleague or offer more space and resources to another. This process appears to skirt obstacles, but it actually uncovers the subtle complications or unrecognised difficulties that hinder performance. It can reduce the extent to which individuals underestimate the performance of other colleagues and minimise employees' resentment if they do not receive a bonus.

These incentive schemes are not a tool to enhance only motivation — they can influence the entire culture of organisations. For example, employees who seldom socialise with managers and would be expected to receive unfair benefits, should occasionally receive a promotion. Employees thus become less likely to believe that decisions are biased or to assume that politics dictate success. This presumption of fairness and equity has been shown to reduce the incidence of stress and aggression in the workplace (e.g., Vigoda, 2002).

Finally, to increase the likelihood that employees perceive the system of reward and bonuses as just, managers should collect anecdotes, articles, or books about successful executives who were inferior or unfortunate in some facet of their life. Perhaps these executives were unable to devote any time to their family life or were afflicted with a psychiatric disorder. These anecdotes should be stored in a database, together with the instances in which they could be relevant. For example, the executive who was unable to devote any time to his family life could be described during a discussion on workload. The executive who endured a psychiatric disorder could be related during a workshop on mental illness.

According to recent research, when employees hear anecdotes or tales that describe a miserable, duplicitous executive or a destitute but content and sincere person, their belief that society is fair and just is reinforced (Kay & Jost, 2003). They hence become more likely to perceive their organisation, as well as the system of rewards and benefits, as fair and just.

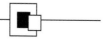

One of the most established principles in psychology is that reward is generally more effective than punishment. However, before incentives and rewards are distributed, workgroups should convene and discuss the obstacles that hindered each individual as well as identify potential solutions.

Unfulfilled Targets

Of course, not every employee can be awarded a bonus or reward. Employees who do not fulfil these goals could obviously feel disillusioned, unmotivated or unconfident. The reactions of managers may exacerbate, rather than ameliorate, these feelings. They may aggravate the doubts and concerns of employees, despite intentions to the contrary.

An example of ludicrous management behaviour was observed in one Australian IT company which for obvious reasons we shall not name. Contrary to company instructions, none of the employees of one department had fastened their computers to the desk as a means to prevent theft. To highlight the potential repercussions of this oversight, the CEO entered the building that night, seized all the computers and conveyed this equipment to his home. Unfortunately, he suddenly became ill and for the next two weeks the organisation was forced to function without those computers.

Usually, however, the reactions of managers to unfulfilled goals and targets seem plausible and reasonable but nevertheless may provoke a sequence of unintended complications. For example, when employees fail to reach their targets, managers will strive to offer support. They may ascribe the shortfalls of this employee to factors that could not have been prevented — destructive management practices, unfair performance evaluations, politics, misfortune and so on. 'It's not your fault — the instructions were unclear' or 'Don't worry, you were just unlucky' are ubiquitous examples.

But, some provocative scientific studies reveal these excuses do not motivate employees (Levy, Cawley, & Foti, 1998). Indeed, these excuses amplify the doubts, cynicism and sense of impotence that employees experience. They merely demonstrate that forces the employees cannot control might obstruct their performance, leading them to feel helpless, unmotivated and stressed. Managers should instead identify tactics and strategies the employees could have applied to circumvent these obstacles.

In addition, many managers monitor the activities and outcomes of these employees more closely. They observe employees who do not realise their targets more often. Some astonishing research has nevertheless revealed that such surveillance tends to actually reduce effort (Witowski & Streinsmeier-Pelster, 1998). Employees who feel unconfident and helpless do not want to be perceived as incompetent or unskilled. They may withdraw their effort or reduce their concentration. Subsequent failures can be ascribed to effort, not ability; to motivation, not skill. When these employees are not monitored closely, they do not feel the need to withdraw their effort.

To address this difficulty, after employees fail to fulfil a target, their behaviour and performance should not be monitored. Instead, they should be granted the opportunity to specify when they would like their performance to be appraised. To further promote effort, managers should create a database in which they record all the excuses that are used to exonerate shortfalls or to justify failures — such as late nights, limited preparation or dysfunctional equipment. Employees should then be encouraged to set goals that preclude these excuses. They could be asked to retain a journal that chronicles their sleep patterns, preparation before meetings, maintenance of equipment and many other activities. Managers should consult this journal during performance evaluations.

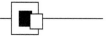

Managers should grant more autonomy to employees who failed to fulfil their goals and targets, at least for a few weeks.

Criticism and Feedback

Employees who do not perform effectively or behave appropriately sometimes need to receive guidance, feedback, or even criticism. Criticism can either inspire or destroy the confidence of employees; it can either enrich or reduce the performance of these individuals. Therefore, feedback, especially unfavourable feedback, must be offered cautiously and appropriately.

Criticism can damage the motivation of individual employees and the performance of workgroups. For example, after employees receive unfair criticism, they tend to identify the flaws in this feedback, the shortfalls of their manager and the problems of the organisation. They might exhibit disdain or merely disregard their manager altogether. Research reveals that employees who demonstrate this disdain towards colleagues and managers subsequently perform less productively, vigorously and efficiently. Evidence of this aspect appeared in a fascinating study conducted by Ciarocco, Summer and Baumeister (2001).

Participants undertook a variety of activities; for example, some individuals had earlier been encouraged to evade another participant. Individuals who had been told not to interact with another participant demonstrated less persistence in the activities they performed. The mental processes that are activated to evade, shun, or disdain another person tend to reduce the effort that individuals can devote to work activities.

Many managers believe that criticism is more effective and consequential than praise. They believe that employees should be able to accommodate — and even embrace — unfavourable feedback. They believe that employees will improve only when they receive the appropriate criticism. For example, in an Australian company, an employee was instructed to read the 'mistakes book' as soon as she arrived each day. In this 'mistakes book' her supervisor had recorded every trivial error, oversight and shortfall that she had perpetrated the day before.

Unfortunately, managers who frequently criticise their employees impair performance on a broad range of activities. Employees focus their attention on the issues in which they have been criticised recently and withdraw effort from other behaviours. Furthermore, their confidence diminishes, their blood pressure rises and their health deteriorates (Begley, Lee, & Czajka, 2000).

Indeed, criticisms can exacerbate the problems they were intended to address. When employees feel unconfident, helpless, or detached, they tend to withdraw from their job and often arrive late to work. Every time they arrive late, they will receive disapproval and condemnation from their increasingly frustrated managers. Nevertheless, whenever their punctuality is criticised, they feel even more unconfident and useless (Koslowsky, Sagie, Krausz, & Singer, 1997). So, they withdraw even further and may arrive increasingly late. They might not even arrive at all.

Managers who offer feedback and criticisms must circumvent these hurdles. First, they need to identify the strengths of their subordinates that may be subtle but vital or that few of their colleagues recognise. Perhaps managers can identify the advantages or unexpected benefits of the idiosyncrasies of their subordinates. For example, managers should recognise that confronting, forthright employees tend to forge progress and development. Impulsive employees can reach complex decisions rapidly and often effectively; unmethodical employees tend to be more creative and innovative. Managers should be aware that reserved employees tend to be more reflective, but are nevertheless more considered and thoughtful. Once managers highlight these strengths and benefits, their subordinates will not perceive them as misguided and will not challenge the credibility or insight of these managers.

Managers should also confine their criticisms to vital, not peripheral, issues — especially if the employees are not especially confident (Seta, Donaldson, & Seta, 1999). They should not criticise behaviours, customs, or inclinations that do not undermine performance nor denounce tendencies or habits they perceive as annoying or frustrating — unless these behaviours impinge on productivity and efficiency.

For example, one manager once distributed a memorandum to all employees that stated, 'To the persons who find it funny to repeatedly position my Star Wars figurines in inappropriate positions, please stop … I find this extremely distasteful and offensive … If this continues, I will report this to HR'. Managers who criticise inconsequential behaviours are more likely to be perceived as misguided rather than credible (Rudawsky, Lungren, & Grasha, 1999).

Instead, managers should convene a meeting to discuss the career plans, goals, hopes and aspirations of their employees. In these meetings, they should identify the behaviours or shortfalls of the subordinates that could obstruct these objectives. Subordinates will not dismiss these criticisms as trivial or inconsequential and will not discount feedback that relates to their primary objectives.

Managers should work to exhibit a supportive and genuine manner. Most managers try to establish a supportive environment and portray a cooperative tone, but their gestures and facial expressions may belie this attitude. Instead, they may appear uncooperative, aloof or conceited and they need to develop appropriate gestures and suitable facial expressions. To appear compelling, but cooperative, managers need to exhibit a range of behaviours. These include: leaning forwards, nodding their head, laughing, tilting their head, placing a hand on the back of another person, smiling, or speaking loudly — rather than blinking, chewing their lips, shrugging their shoulders, forming a fist, lowering their eyebrows, narrowing their eyes, pointing, speaking in a monotone, having a quavering voice or whispering (Rashotte, 2002). Research reveals that managers who display inappropriate gestures and facial expressions appear equally discourteous, regardless of whether or not they praise or castigate the subordinate.

Managers are also more likely to seem impolite, aloof or detached when they feel a sense of shame or guilt. Many managers experience this guilt when they reproach their employees, encourage them to address some fault, prescribe further training to these employees, or revoke some of the autonomy and authority these employees currently enjoy. They are especially likely to experience this guilt — to endure this shame — if they feel they might have impeded these employees.

These managers attempt to alleviate their sense of shame and to minimise their guilt by attempting to provide the feedback as rapidly as possible (Folger & Skarlicki, 1998). They try to blame the employees and to cultivate antipathy towards these individuals by attempting to excuse their behaviour and to mitigate their unease. In other words, we do not mistreat other individuals when they have erred, but we do mistreat these individuals when we have erred. Perhaps the most extreme example of rapid negative feedback would be the employee who recently received a text message on her mobile telephone from her manager, which read, 'You have just been dismissed — sorry'.

Folger and Skarlicki (1998) undertook a delightful simulation that revealed the behaviour of managers when they experience guilt. Participants had to pretend to retrench another individual. As part of this simulation, some of the participants had earlier been told their own incompetence had accelerated the need to retrench individuals because they had not attracted enough clients. Other participants had earlier been told that market demands had plummeted. Participants who were told their own incompetence had accelerated the impending redundancy displayed an aloof, bitter manner when they dismissed another person. Even in a laboratory setting, an artificial simulation, the guilt of managers inadvertently influenced their behaviour during dismissals.

Employees are often criticised during appraisals of their performance. Immediately before these meetings, employees should first be asked to list many of their qualities and attributes, such as 'I am ambitious' or 'I am proficient in mathematics'. Employees should then rate the extent they believe they are granted opportunities to utilise these qualities and attributes in the workplace. Finally, together with their supervisor, they should identify roles they could assume in the future to utilise these qualities. After this process, employees become more receptive to criticism (Dijksterhuis, 2004).

In a significant study that verified the value of this procedure, some individuals read a list of desirable traits, such as 'warm' or 'smart', each of which was preceded by the letter 'I'. They then performed a sequence of activities and their performance was criticised. Relative to other participants, these individuals were more likely to concur with the criticisms they received (Dijksterhuis, 2004). Specifically, over time, individuals develop an unconscious catalogue of their qualities and deficiencies. After individuals read or write a list of desirable traits, each of which is preceded by the letter 'I', these deficiencies dissipate. Although unaware of this change, individuals thus develop a more favourable image of themselves, which has been demonstrated to foster resilience to criticism. Managers who offer overt praise, however, do not significantly impinge on this unconscious catalogue — overt praise, therefore, does not foster resilience to subsequent criticisms (Brown, Farnham, & Cook, 2002).

Some employees are more receptive to criticisms and feedback than are other individuals. Managers should publicise the characteristics of defensive individuals. They should highlight the irony that confident and cooperative individuals, who do not need to receive extensive feedback are usually the most receptive to criticism. They should emphasise that competitive, manipulative individuals dismiss criticism and behave defensively and that only individuals who believe they can improve and can progress are receptive to criticism.

Finally, to reduce the incidence of superfluous criticisms, hierarchies need to be banished or refined. Hierarchies imply that some individuals are superior to others and also promote criticism as individuals strive to secure a superior position (Allan & Gilbert, 2002). To temper these hierarchies, managers need to ensure the rank and status of employees varies across domains. Employees who receive authority in one role should not be given authority in another. Employees who have not progressed significantly along the management path should be assigned to positions of leadership in various committees, project teams and so forth. The lines of authority can thus remain clear, without the hierarchies that foster criticisms.

Before a manager presents criticisms, they should ask each employee to identify their strengths as well as future positions, roles and opportunities to utilise these qualities. Carefully constructed criticisms should be directed towards behaviours or inclinations that should be redressed before these opportunities are explored.

Conflict Resolution

Even when criticisms are presented sensitively, disappointment, disagreements and disputes will persist. Indeed, attempts to curb these conflicts and to minimise disagreement can create an undercurrent of resentment, frustration and ultimately disunity.

Nevertheless, scientific findings suggest that conflicts and disagreements should not be shunned, suppressed or circumvented (Friedman, Tidd, Currall, & Tsai, 2000). For instance, when employee unions are too cooperative or too accommodating, employees have been demonstrated to actually be less likely to receive sufficient training and resources (Bacon & Blyton, 2002). The unions are less likely to secure these developmental opportunities.

However, some organisations successfully support the unions — perhaps by offering training in negotiation, employee relations, safety and remuneration to union delegates. They might encourage employees to enrol in a union or equip unions with premises, stationery or equipment, such as computers. Employees in these organisations do not feel the need to support the union over management or vice versa (see Martin & Sinclair, 2001). They do not feel the need to devote all their loyalty to the union or to engage in every instance of industrial action. Thus disputes and conflicts become less acrimonious and less consequential.

In addition, many studies reveal that workgroups in which conflicts are scarce tend to be less progressive and innovative. Workgroups that comprise sociable, popular, accommodating individuals tend to suppress their disagreements and thus stifle creativity, development and improvement. In contrast, workgroups that embrace conflicts, engage in debates, address disputes and encourage disagreements tend to promote innovation. They seek solutions that accommodate conflicting needs and beliefs and thus promote original, novel and effective suggestions. The most effective measure to prevent future conflict is to resolve conflict suitably and manage disputes.

Conflicts should centre on work operations and strategies, not individuals. These disputes could revolve around the methods that will be used to complete work, coordinate tasks, monitor quality or publicise the output. Disagreements should obviously not centre on the shortfalls, deficiencies, or habits of individuals, neither explicitly nor tacitly.

Nevertheless, employees struggle to maintain a focus on tasks, not individuals. For example, individuals who feel somewhat unconfident or helpless tend to ascribe conflicts or disagreements to the shortcomings of other individuals, especially individuals they do not like. They believe the dispute would not have arisen had the other individual been competent and informed; had the other individual demonstrated understanding and consideration. This condemnation of other individuals offsets their limited confidence. But, this condemnation of other individuals has also been found to nullify and even reverse the effect of conflicts on creativity. Conflicts that revolve around individuals, not work, tend to stifle innovation.

Several other factors determine whether or not conflicts will be ascribed to the deficits perceived in the other individual. For example, roles that involve negotiation and mediation tend to be assigned to sociable, confident and extraverted individuals. Research, however, challenges this practice as, during negotiations, extraverted individuals are often blamed when conflicts arise. These individuals are often perceived as dominant, assertive and authoritative. The other parties will often perceive this dominance as disruptive, rigid and as the principal source of conflict.

Accordingly, extraverted employees need to curb this dominating impression. They need to disclose their agenda, needs and concerns openly. They should seek advice from the other party in relation to how they should resolve their predicament and should exhibit respect, not authority.

Second, during conflicts and disputes, individuals often feel frustration, dissatisfaction or even fury. Some individuals will attempt to show this resentment to intimidate and influence their opponent. This indignation, according to some enlightening research, undermines the benefits to both themselves and the other party (Conlon & Hunt, 2002). If individuals experience powerful emotions during conflicts, they will tend to feel anxiety, resentment, irritation and pressure and experience unpleasant emotions. According to recent studies, when individuals experience unpleasant emotions, they typically focus their attention upon unfavourable events and attributes. They might perceive a compliment they receive as manipulative rather than genuine or an assertion as distorted rather than accurate. Their trust towards their opposition diminishes; they do not collaborate, compromise or seek resolutions that accommodate both parties — they do not progress.

However, no conflicts are innocuous. No solution can resolve every issue or problem that lurks below the surface. But, many employees — and indeed many managers — expect that such negotiations will facilitate future discussions and perhaps even preclude subsequent frustrations and conflicts. They expect that mediation sessions will purge all the under-lying tensions and problems.

But, scientists have uncovered some staggering and sobering findings, which underscore the problems that arise even when conflicts and disagreements are resolved effectively (Maxham & Netemeyer, 2002). These studies reveal that employees become even more sensitive to further conflicts and more disturbed by future disputes after problems and difficul-ties are resolved effectively. Specifically, after conflicts are resolved, subsequent disputes violate the expectation of cus-tomers that all the issues had been settled and resolved. So, these additional conflicts provoke considerable anxiety, resent-ment and disappointment.

To demonstrate, Maxham and Netemeyer (2002) con-ducted a study to investigate the expectations and attitudes of bank customers who had complained on two separate occasions. Before and after each complaint, customers com-pleted a survey that assessed their satisfaction with the bank.

In addition, customers completed another survey that established the extent to which they felt these complaints had been resolved effectively. Relative to the other participants, customers who believed the first complaint had been resolved efficiently and professionally were especially critical of their bank after the second complaint. That is, after the bank had resolved the first issue effectively, customers had expected improved services in the future and were thus especially dissatisfied when an additional error arose.

A series of suggestions can be considered to address these complications. First, conflicts should not proceed if either party feels anger, hostility or aggression — one of the parties should propose they postpone the argument. The argument should then continue over email — an environment that tends to moderate emotions — until both parties agree to reconvene in person (Dorado, et al., 2002). All disputes must ultimately be settled in person, however, to ensure the issues are resolved actively rather than disregarded altogether.

In addition, to further moderate emotions, managers and their subordinates should learn to apply humour during conflicts and disputes. Humour has been demonstrated to promote innovative, effective solutions to work problems, difficulties and disputes (e.g., Domino, Short, Evans, & Romano, 2002). Managers and employees should record amusing comments that other individuals express during meetings and discussions. They should then consider how these comments could be applied to other situations. For example, some comments might involve exaggeration of one possible outcome; others might involve the integration of alternative proposals to create an amusing, but implausible solution.

Finally, employees should monitor their emotions during conflicts. They should note any emotions they feel. They should transcribe the angst, anguish, anger and anxiety they experience and also the thoughts that coincide with these emotions. They should write down the events that ignite these emotions. Finally, perhaps most importantly, they should defer any attempts to resolve these feelings until after the meeting or discussion has been terminated.

In short, conflicts need to be resolved actively, cooperatively, dispassionately and rationally. Anxiety, irritation and stress need to be tempered; but, perhaps the most destructive emotion in the context of conflicts is anger.

> *During any fiery discussions, employees should monitor and memorise the events that triggered anxiety or anger. After the discussion, they should specify three activities they could undertake to redress these emotions. This exercise minimises the likelihood that unpleasant emotions will amplify the conflict.*

Aggression

Everyone has witnessed the employees and managers who display anger. Anger and aggression can impair flexibility, negotiation, empathy, trust and judgment — creating instead a sense of certainty, a sense of conviction (Teidens & Linton, 2001). When individuals experience this certainty and conviction, they tend to engage in risky, hazardous acts. They might invest imprudently, breach safety regulations or even harm colleagues.

Indeed, some aggressive, callous but charming employees feel no guilt or shame when they offend, harm or abuse another person. Aggressive employees are unable to recognise sadness and fear in other individuals. In one series of studies, researchers articulated several neutral words, such as 'carpet' with a variety of tones or emotions. First, a happy tone was portrayed, then an angry tone, a disgusted tone, a fearful tone and a sad tone. In contrast to other employees, ruthless but charming individuals misconstrued sad or fearful tones as happy, angry or disgusted (Blair, et al.,

2002). They plainly could not decipher sadness or fear in other individuals.

A few organisations actually favour aggressive employees. In one security firm, a male struck and assaulted a female recruiter when his application to join the company was rejected. The next day, the CEO — perhaps impressed by this torrent of hostility — overturned the decision and actually employed the applicant. The majority of organisations, however, strive to curb rather than encourage aggression.

Regrettably, managers often do not know how to respond when a subordinate, peer, superior or customer exhibits aggression and hostility. For example, some managers will act immediately to quell or subdue the aggression of subordinates. They might penalise the individual without delay or immediately demonstrate disdain or disappointment.

According to some scientific findings, this impulsive behaviour merely reinforces the inclinations of aggressive individuals (Mikulay & Goffin, 1998). It merely demonstrates that impulsive reactions to adversity — the cornerstone of aggression — is prevalent and justifiable. In short, this behaviour merely raises the likelihood the individual will respond aggressively in the future.

Managers should therefore first delay their responses to acts of aggression. Specifically, to foster the ability of aggressive individuals to compromise and collaborate, managers should convene meetings in which employees express a variety of strategies to overcome workplace issues and improve performance. Aggressive individuals should later be asked to integrate these solutions into a single, unified, coherent proposal — a proposal that all colleagues accept and embrace. This attempt to reconcile the conflicting opinions of other employees can promote flexibility, forge adaptability and foster versatility — the archenemies of aggression (see DeChurch & Marks, 2001).

Second, managers need to build a workplace that prevents further aggression. For example, they should convene a discussion on the health and welfare of employees that includes information about exercise, stress, fatigue and related topics. During this discussion, managers should determine whether employees believe that anger should be expressed and released, or concealed and quashed.

Even though many popular handbooks recommend that anger should be vented, managers should reveal that recent studies show that anger expression can be harmful, damaging and destructive (Bushman, Baumeister, & Phillips, 2001). Blood pressure rises dramatically, relationships deteriorate and individuals become more likely to adopt hostile attitudes towards colleagues in the future.

So, anger should not be released and hostility should not be expressed (see also Wenzlaff & Bates, 2000). Instead, these emotions need to be supplanted and overshadowed with thoughts that reflect conflicting feelings. They should consider the intentions of any individual to whom they feel anger. They should identify, and even feel, the concerns and anxiety this individual might have experienced, perhaps even visualising a scene they hope to achieve in several years. All these images alleviate aggression — both now and in the future.

Finally, managers often need to placate employees after a specific incident. Sometimes, employees are enraged after they do not receive a bonus or frustrated after they receive a criticism. To alleviate this frustration, managers should determine whether or not some of the blame could be ascribed to these individuals themselves. Perhaps the employees could have worked more diligently or studied more extensively. If so, these employees should be encouraged to articulate sentences that include the term 'I'.

Whenever employees demonstrate resentment towards another individual, they should be asked to consider how they would have acted differently to this person.

For example, these individuals could be asked, 'How would you have acted differently if you were granted my role?' According to recent studies, after employees express sentences that comprise the term 'I', they immediately assume a sense of responsibility. They immediately experience a sense of duty — rather than ascribe errors, problems and shortfalls to the incompetence or negligence of other individuals (Neumann, 2000).

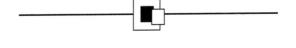

Chapter 6

Promoting Employee Wellbeing

Safety

There are numerous factors needing consideration to promote general employee welfare. As seen in the previous chapter, aggression can be an obvious risk to health and safety, but complacency can be an equally unsafe practice. Employees may not seem concerned that safety hazards pervade many work environments. They may not seem too disturbed by the heavy objects, unstable chairs, elevated surfaces, electrical currents, toxic chemicals, open flames, slippery floors, sharp edges, dim lights, glare, noise and extreme temperatures that may be present.

However, some managers never seem to be able to eradicate, or even reduce, the frequency of safety incidents and breaches. Many of the programs that organisations institute to improve safety are futile and policies formulated to improve safety are ineffective. These programs and policies do not abolish the barriers that impede safe practices or address the mechanisms that promote risk.

For instance, individuals may perceive themselves as more cautious, careful and responsible than their colleagues. Through the media, they hear of reckless acts and risks taken by others. They witness hazardous motorists and thus believe they drive more safely and speed less than average. Anecdotes about foolhardy employees make them believe they work more cautiously than average.

Most employees believe they are more circumspect than other individuals and that safety campaigns are not directed towards them. Safety campaigns thus tend to be disregarded and may be perceived as extraneous, not vital. Indeed, after an accident, employees perceive themselves as unfortunate and other individuals as incompetent.

Walton and McKeown (2001) conducted a powerful series of studies to highlight these issues. A broad spectrum of drivers were asked to estimate whether or not they drive more rapidly than an average motorist. They were also presented with a series of advertising slogans used in earlier campaigns to improve road safety. Participants were asked to recall the medium — TV, radio, or print — in which they had previously encountered this campaign.

Most of the participants claimed to drive less rapidly than an average motorist. In actuality, approximately 50% of individuals drive less rapidly than an average motorist. Furthermore, relative to other participants, drivers who claimed to drive slower than an average motorist were less likely to recall the safety campaigns. In other words, individuals who overrate their own performance tend to disregard safety campaigns.

Some programs attempt to shock the audience with a graphic demonstration of the trauma, pain or destruction that can occur when individuals behave unsafely and irresponsibly. They assume that shock tactics will instigate safe practices. Yet studies have refuted this intuition (Ben-Ari, Florian, & Mikulincer, 2000) and show that shocking, graphic portrayals can actually increase the rate of accidents. When individuals watch a graphic film that depicts an accident, they feel a sense of threat and a sense of anxiety. To alleviate this threat, these individuals try to reassert their dominance and confidence. Some employees may perceive risky acts as an opportunity to reclaim this dominance and that hazardous behaviour is admirable and commanding. Therefore, they engage in risky acts to redeem their pride, dignity and confidence. These employees are thus more susceptible to incidents after they watch a graphic film or campaign.

Furthermore, the usual pattern for organisations to present safety programs simultaneously to all employees in the workgroup may not be the best approach. Scientists have demonstrated this practice is not optimal (Hui, Lam, & Schaubroeck, 2001). Safety programs should be first presented to cooperative, supportive employees who are seen to be genuine and considerate, rather than manipulative or egocentric. These individuals are not considered to be motivated by ulterior motives or hidden agendas and their behaviour is seen to be appropriate and respectable. Their colleagues are more likely to mimic their behaviour and to emulate their compliance with regulations, their prevention of incidents, their vigilance with equipment and their communication with supervisors.

While many organisations implement training programs to prevent accidents, they may not eradicate the hazards — elevated surfaces, toxic chemicals, open flames, sharp edges, dim lights may remain. For example, unsuitable, cramped work conditions can lead to employees' postural problems. Likewise, some clothing manufacturers concede that they apply formaldehyde to their garments — a toxic preservative. Employees who process the clothes before they are distributed therefore inhale formaldehyde fumes. Training programs are thus intended to minimise the deleterious effects of these hazards and to promote practices that prevent accidents.

Studies have indicated though that training programs without a concomitant reduction in hazards tend to be futile (Brown, Willis, & Prussia, 2000). Participants recognise that many of the safety hazards persist. They assume that senior managers do not perceive safety as vital, significant and imperative — therefore, neither do the participants of these programs. Hence, they will seldom follow the guidelines or conform to safety standards, comply with safety policies or observe the safety regulations.

To promote safety, some managers may threaten to punish employees who breach regulations or disregard policies. Employees who do not comply with these policies forfeit bonuses and promotions as well as receive severe reprimands.

Punitive actions have been scientifically demonstrated to promote violations of the safety policies rather than foster compliance. As a consequence of the threats they receive and the associated apprehension they experience, employees focus on their immediate duties and responsibilities rather than future objectives. Employees who focus on immediate, rather than remote, goals tend to disregard the future consequences of their actions. They seek instant gratification; hence, they paradoxically disregard safety regulations, which they feel merely hinder their pleasure (Zimbardo, Keough, & Boyd, 1997).

To cultivate a safe environment, managers must first demonstrate the importance of future objectives. For example, managers should consider the acts that employees undertook many years before when they allocate bonuses and promotions. Achievements reached many years ago should be rewarded, and support demonstrated in the past should also be recognised.

Safety messages without concomitant attention to physical hazards are unlikely to be effective. Furthermore, employees who seem cooperative, supportive and productive should be invited to follow new safety policies before these regulations are publicised to everyone else.

Safety campaigns should be tailored to the unique attributes, motivations and interests of each employee. For instance, sociable, extraverted individuals are more likely to act unsafely if their job is monotonous, repetitive and unstimulating

(Cooper, Agocha, & Sheldon, 2000). Anxious, sensitive individuals are more likely to engage in risks if they feel threatened, insecure and uncertain. Thus, extraverted employees need to be assigned roles that involve interactions with a diverse array of individuals. Anxious employees need to be assigned roles in which they receive autonomy and independence as well as support and guidance.

Counselling and Support

Even the best safety campaigns cannot guarantee the health and welfare of all employees at all times. When incidents, misfortune and adversity arise, managers therefore need to perform several distinct roles concurrently. They may need to seek assistance, coordinate responses, allocate tasks and convene discussions. Their most difficult and important role, perhaps, is to provide support, guidance and counselling to the individuals who feel upset, disturbed, afraid or angry.

Yet, many managers struggle with this role and find it difficult to alleviate the anguish, confusion and distress of other individuals. Indeed, few managers are able to overcome their own anguish, confusion and distress effectively and appropriately. Instead, managers may assume, or at least convince themselves, that employees will be able to cope with the difficulties and afflictions they experience at work or home. They may believe that such problems will not persist or that they are not especially devastating

A wealth of research has highlighted the fallacy of this assumption (e.g., Blantan, Axsom, McClive, & Price, 2001). Studies show that managers underestimate the grief, disquiet or suffering that other individuals experience and overestimate individuals' ability to overcome this anguish. As a consequence, they believe they will not need to intervene or assist and convince themselves that perhaps a demonstration of concern or a few words of encouragement should suffice.

One such research program involved participants being asked to estimate the extent to which they expect to feel shock and anguish after they experience various adversities — such as cancer or retrenchment. On a separate occasion, they were asked to estimate the extent to which other individuals would experience the same emotions. Most participants believed they would experience more suffering than would other individuals (Blantan, Axsom, McClive, & Price, 2001).

To elaborate, when individuals consider their own misfortunes, they imagine all the difficulties, complications and obstacles to recovery — the anguish of parents, their responsibility to their children and so forth. But, they are less likely to imagine the complications that other individuals would experience in response to the same events. Indeed, some managers may convince themselves the victims were themselves to blame and that they should have prevented this misfortune and overcome their grief.

Managers may also feel that other individuals could provide the best support and guidance to distressed employees — that family, friends, counsellors, or peers are more suited to this role. Research by Settoon and Adkins (1997), however, disputes this assumption. Studies show that employees who rely on friends, family, or counsellors to provide assistance in response to issues and misfortunes at work are less likely to restore their confidence and satisfaction. They are less likely to feel secure at work in the future or to remain committed to the organisation. Family, friends and counsellors do not understand the subtle values, culture and customs of the organisation and hence seldom provide optimal advice.

Finally, managers may try to convince themselves that distressed employees can still be effective and productive and that distress will not hinder workplace performance. Scientific studies indicate otherwise. Even disciplined, diligent, committed, model employees work less efficiently and less productively when distressed. They seem distracted and become susceptible to safety incidents (Iverson & Erwin, 1997). They may persevere inordinately on tasks they cannot complete and cannot overcome these undesirable behaviours.

Managers, thus, will need to assume the role of a counsellor — a role for which they have seldom received training. Managers may inadvertently exacerbate rather than alleviate distress. For example, when counselling an employee, managers seldom focus upon specific events. Unconfident employees are rarely encouraged to discuss a specific instance in they experienced grave doubts in their ability. Stressed employees are seldom prompted to discuss a specific occasion in which they felt overwhelmed.

In fact, managers may feel that specific events are not informative enough and that they are too personal or invasive. Instead, they prefer to blend these events together. They might ask, 'When do you usually feel least confident?' rather than 'Describe one occasion in which you felt especially unconfident'. The latest scientific findings suggest this neglect of specific instances inhibits progress (Phillippot, Schaefer, & Herbette, 2003). Instead, employees should be asked to strive to recall a specific, distinct and upsetting episode in their lives. To recall these events, employees must effectively reconstruct the episode by reassembling the event using memory, logic, inference and careful reflection. They might infer they experienced grave doubts in their confidence after they received unfavourable feedback or that they experienced pronounced anxiety after they received additional responsibilities they could not fulfil.

Research tells us that to reconstruct these distressing episodes, humans have evolved to spontaneously subdue emotions that would disrupt their concentration. They inadvertently suppress anxiety and curb their melancholy. They subjugate any emotion that could impede the reconstruction of this event, and therefore they feel more enthused, content and tolerant.

Indeed, when managers encourage an employee to reflect closely upon their emotions, the employees' shame often abates and their confusion diminishes. A sense of perspective emerges and a sense of hope appears. Yet, not always. Studies suggest this approach can be fraught with pitfalls (Kelly,

Klusas, von Weiss, & Kenny, 2001). As employees delve further into their emotions, they form new memories of their anguish, anger, despair, panic or their confusion. On each occasion they recall the incident, or encounter a similar event, the same intense feelings will arise and so their grief intensifies rather than abates.

After a traumatic event, individuals form mental images of the various visions, sounds, and thoughts that coincided with this event in an effort to understand the trauma. These mental images provoke the emotions the individuals experienced while the event unfolded, and thus they relive their pain, shock, panic and distress.

Some managers, however, believe that employees should focus exclusively on pleasant events — holidays, celebrations or victories — rather than traumatic events. Yet studies have demonstrated that employees should not focus solely on pleasant events (e.g., Smyth, 1998). Instead, they should be encouraged to write about some traumatic event they experienced, such as a recent divorce. They should write several pages about their feelings, thoughts, memories, and images. This exercise converts their painful memories into detached insights. They become less likely to relive the sounds, visions, pain, and distress they experienced.

Finally, to establish rapport and trust in counselling, some managers are taught to mirror the gestures and posture of the person with whom they are interacting. They might tap one of their fingers, stroke their chin or fondle their hair whenever the other person engages in one of these behaviours. This approach can indeed promote rapport and trust if used subtley and sensitively.

Yet some gestures and postures should definitely not be mirrored (e.g., Tiedens & Fragale, 2003), as they can undermine relationships and destroy trust. For example, when employees exhibit an unguarded posture — perhaps with their legs apart and one arm placed on the top of an empty chair — they feel threatened when managers adopt a similar position. Likewise, when employees exhibit a cramped position — with their legs together and their hands rested on their thighs — they again feel threatened when managers adopt a comparable position. An unguarded posture represents a sense of dominance, a sense of authority, whereas a cramped position represents a submissive and accommodating demeanour. Humans have evolved to feel threatened whenever they encounter someone who exhibits the same level of dominance as themselves.

Managers who provide support and counselling thus need to make use of a series of techniques. First, they should ascertain whether the individual actually needs emotional support or practical advice. Does the individual want to receive empathy, understanding, warmth, comfort or relief? Or would the individual prefer practical advice, guidance, ideas, plans or inspiration? Individuals who want emotional support but receive practical advice, or vice versa, tend to become even more frustrated (Horowitz, et al., 2001). They can feel misunderstood, mistreated and patronised. Individuals who emphasise their feelings or discuss personal concerns usually seek emotional support. Those who highlight their performance or discuss work tasks usually seek practical advice.

Second, to provide emotional support, managers should encourage the individuals to clarify their feelings, rather than giving details of the event that provoked the problem. They could ask, 'Do you feel upset and angry?' or 'Do you feel dizzy and faint?', not, 'How did the other people react?' or 'How many people were present?'. Managers should also emphasise they would also feel upset, frustrated, concerned and confused in response to the same event. They should not trivialise the incident to pacify the employee. They should assert, 'It makes me frustrated as well', not, 'You'll be right. It's only a minor incident' or 'Other employees have endured much more serious problems before'.

Third, when employees seek guidance to resolve some ongoing emotional issue, such as limited confidence, they should be encouraged to describe specific events. For example, they could be asked to discuss a specific occasion in which they felt unconfident. Employees can address issues more effectively after they describe specific episodes. Employees who have recently experienced a traumatic event should be asked to write about the emotions, the thoughts, the sounds and the images they experienced during this event. They should write about this event once a week, over the course of one or two months. Nevertheless, they should be warned that this process could initially provoke distress, but will eventually alleviate these unpleasant emotions.

Fourth, managers should also emphasise the strengths, qualities and attributes of these individuals that could be used to address the issue. They could suggest, 'You always seem to be aware of your feelings and this insight should help you', or 'You seem to have developed a broad network of friends to support you'. Managers could also describe a similar experience they had resolved many years ago — perhaps a divorce, a retrenchment or a demotion — to demonstrate their empathy and understanding. However, they should concede their experiences were not equivalent and that they recognise each experience is unique.

If employees seek practical advice, focussing their attention upon performance, productivity and success at work, managers should refrain from any exploration of emotions and feelings. They should instead provide practical and rational advice, perhaps by offering guidance or insights. These insights may have been gleaned from discussions with peers, observations at work, or previous literature. Effective managers could construct a database in which they store and share all the insights and practices they have discovered that can enhance behaviour, bolster emotions and improve performance.

For example, they might record an insight derived from a training program in which they were asked to specify conflicting traits in their friends and colleagues. One of their friends might be empathic on some occasions but ruthless or aloof in other situations. One of their colleagues might exhibit confidence, even conceit, in some settings but panic and shame on other days. When employees recognise and appreciate conflicting traits in the same person, they seldom overreact to minor instances of discourtesy, sarcasm or irritability (Lopez, 2001).

In contrast, when employees do not recognise that individuals can be multifaceted they may overreact to minor incidents (Lopez, 2001). After some minor quarrel, they might suddenly perceive a colleague as hostile, as irrational or even repugnant. The person had not changed; but the perception of this person has been debased irreparably.

Alternatively and perhaps preferably, managers should invite and encourage employees to uncover their own insights, solutions and resolutions. The key is to ensure that employees identify many possible solutions and avenues to resolve their problems, even if these suggestions seem impractical, implausible or improbable. To generate these solutions, employees should reverse some facet of another suggestion or integrate disparate proposals. For example, consider an employee who would like to earn more credibility and respect in their workgroup. They could decide to present a seminar or convene a discussion to introduce some of their unique insights, talents, experiences and perspective. Next, they could reverse one facet of this suggestion — perhaps they could present their shortfalls instead or listen rather than present. They could write a memorandum rather than present a speech or they could ask their colleagues to identify their own shortfalls and limitations.

Employees should then identify the benefits or outcomes that each solution yields. They should extract the key features of each suggestion — those that must be maintained to ensure the benefits are achieved. Employees should then integrate these features to form an amalgamated solution. This process might seem cumbersome or artificial, but only when employees defy convention, circumvent their innate tendencies or relinquish their habitual thought patterns will they create innovative and effective solutions to problems. Creative pursuits have been shown to improve mood (Kuhl, 2000).

Nevertheless, to relieve the stress that arises when individuals delay their decisions and explore other avenues, they should first identify one possible course of action. They should stipulate the course of action they will pursue if their exploration into other avenues is not successful.

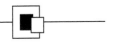

When employees feel upset, distressed and anxious, they should be encouraged to focus on one specific incident. Managers should initially demonstrate empathy. Eventually, however, employees should be encouraged to engage in exercises that promote creativity and identify a diverse range of possible solutions to resolve their issues.

Home Difficulties

Of course managers cannot resolve all the problems and difficulties that employees experience. They cannot redress family illness, divorce, disability and other issues that arise outside the office. Yet, problems at home will significantly impair work performance.

Research shows difficulties at home do not impede all facets of work performance, nor do they disrupt performance on repetitive or practiced tasks. However, they do impair creativity, initiative and any activities that demand original, complex thought processes (Van Dyne, Jehn, & Cummings, 2002). Specifically, family conflicts and problems disrupt subjective, rather than concrete, outcomes. Managers thus need to appreciate the grave effects of family difficulties on workplace performance.

Such problems are unfortunately amplified when employees reach unsuitable decisions. For example, suppose a person needed to decide whether they should accept a tedious, demanding job in which they will receive a $20,000 pay rise or an exciting, enjoyable job in which they will receive only a $10,000 pay rise. Many individuals will select the tedious position to secure the $20,000 pay rise. As Hsee and Zhang (2004) showed, after individuals accept one of these two jobs, the other option gradually fades from memory. They become less aware of the discrepancy between $20,000 and $10,000. The benefits of this tedious job become less prominent and their satisfaction wanes.

To accommodate difficulties at home, many organisations offer special provisions, benefits and policies — such as child-care, flexible work hours, leave options, phased retirement, exercise programs, counselling sessions, re-entry schemes, relocation assistance, and training workshops. Yet, these provisions are not usually granted automatically and instead employees must make applications for such options and may be rejected.

According to some unusual scientific findings, rejections are typically given to employees who supervise other employees, undertake a vital role in the organisation or demonstrate unique skills, insights and abilities (Powell & Mainiero, 1999). In other words, indispensable employees — the same individuals these policies were intended to attract — may not receive provisions to support home life and are thus more likely to leave the organisation.

Yet employees who reach their goals and targets and who enhance workplace performance should be rewarded, rather than penalised. They should be granted more provisions and assistance to address issues at home and not be disadvantaged because they are indispensable. To circumvent this problem, managers need to avoid creating indispensable employees.

Rotation and other training programs should ensure that colleagues can assume the roles of these employees if necessary. Furthermore, managers who do not grant leave or other entitlements to effective employees should be somehow penalised.

Even when managers pursue this approach, employees may feel reluctant to utilise these provisions and benefits. They may feel disadvantaged, uninformed, alienated or lonely. For example, employees who seldom attend the office, such as telecommuters or part-time operators, often feel isolated and unable to influence decisions. So, when they encounter obstacles or uncertainties, they feel helpless and thus stressed and anxious (Igbaria & Guimaraes, 1999). Thus, these individuals should perhaps be encouraged to establish their own committee. They should be invited to institute their own collective in which they explore and address their unique needs. In addition, to be perceived as legitimate rather than peripheral, this committee should also be assigned other issues, such as workplace safety.

Employees themselves can benefit from learning how to reach suitable decisions that will promote satisfaction at work and at home. To illustrate a scheme that optimises decisions, consider employees who need to decide between two options, such as a tedious or an interesting task. Suppose the tedious task can be completed within 45 minutes and the interesting task can be completed within 30 minutes. In addition, suppose they will receive a $200 bonus if they complete the tedious task and a $100 bonus if they complete the interesting task. Under this scheme, the duration can be regarded as a *cost* — any characteristic to be minimised. The bonus can be regarded as a *benefit* — any characteristic to be maximised; and the level of enjoyment can be regarded as a drawback of the tedious task and a benefit of the interesting task. To decide which option to select, individuals should emphasise the attributes that are regarded as a drawback of one alternative and a benefit of the other. For instance, they could primarily focus upon task enjoyment and not the duration

The frequency with which managers grant leave or other entitlements should be monitored. Managers who do not grant leave or entitlements to the most effective employees should be penalised somehow; rewards or recognition could be diminished, for example.

or bonus. As a guideline, these attributes should be regarded as approximately twice as important as the other properties.

Training and Development

While only a limited percentage of organisations offer benefits such as telecommuting, job sharing, sabbaticals and profit shares, most organisations offer some form of training, either to enhance work skills or improve interpersonal behaviour. Training programs have the potential to enrich everyone and yet many training programs do not provide consequential information. Instead they may provide information that participants already know, but perhaps using terms they do not, supplying contentment, not content. The information may not align with the findings of scientific studies and the teaching methods employed may enhance the popularity and reputation of the instructors rather than the knowledge and skills of participants.

Consider the following example on the structure and organisation of training material. The information is organised into distinct sections with each section beginning with a topic heading. The objectives are enumerated with targets and the process of assessment outlined. The relationship between this topic and the previous material is explained and finally, the topic is introduced, perhaps with an amusing anecdote. All of these features impart clarity and satisfy participants.

However, according to research findings that will alarm many educators, all of these features may actually undermine learning (e.g., Towler & Dipboye, 2001). Research now reveals that features that impose a structure and organisation onto the material — topic headings or lists of objectives — may inhibit learning, disrupt comprehension and thus restrict the utility of training programs.

When these features are introduced, participants do not attempt to organise the material themselves or to integrate this material with previous knowledge. They fail to uncover disparities and consistencies with other information or to consider the instances in which this information could be applied. Therefore, these participants cannot apply the information to novel situations or refine the material to accommodate specific needs and demands. The information is retained as static facts rather than fruitful principles. Likewise, extraneous anecdotes during the introduction of a topic have also been shown to disrupt learning (Harp & Mayer, 1998).

In research conducted by Annette Towler and Robert Dipboye in 2001, participants listened to a lecture that had been recorded earlier. Some of the lectures were organised effectively. Topic headings were included, acronyms were excluded, connectives such as 'in contrast' and 'whereas' were utilised to coordinate sentences and the relevance of sections to the overall theme was specified. Other lectures did not incorporate any of these features but were otherwise identical. An examination was then administered where participants utilised this material to solve problems. Participants performed more effectively if they had attended the lecture in which the material was not organised coherently.

Furthermore, to encourage effort and dedication, many training instructors introduce activities to ensure that participants feel accountable. They administer examinations, assess knowledge, evaluate skills, and ask questions. These activities help promote effort but may also produce anxiety.

Individuals who experience this anxiety — this sense of apprehension and tension — strive to minimise errors and difficulties. Hency they attempt to minimise shortfalls and problems, rather than advance their knowledge and expertise. They may shun activities that demand effort but fail to enhance their credibility (Zhang, 2003). For instance, they do not consider how the information applies to their work. They do not integrate the material with previous knowledge but instead learn by rote and memorise details.

The approach that instructors adopt, however, is not the only impediment to learning. The scope or range of these programs is often narrow. In contrast, some employees receive training in skills that could also be utilised in other areas or organisations to that in which they are presently working — perhaps accounting processes, computer programming or leadership styles. This training tends to foster suitable attitudes, elevated motivation and intense concentration. Such training provisions have been shown to promote loyalty, dedication and aid retention.

When employees do not receive these wider generic skills, they feel resigned to their current positions and feel obliged to remain at the organisation. This sense of resignation and obligation tends to exacerbate their stress and to promote defiance rather than compliance. They feel trapped and helpless (Meyer, Stanley, Herscovitch, & Topolnytsky, 2002).

Therefore, when managers or instructors present information, they should first ensure that most, but not all, the material appears in a logical order. They should occasionally switch between topics to facilitate learning, to promote careful analysis and to ensure that students integrate distinct issues into a coherent framework. Managers should then encourage participants to specify their own topic headings after each section is presented. Participants should also be encouraged to ascertain how each topic links to the overall theme. Perhaps, to facilitate this process, managers could provide multiple choices, such as a list of topic headings, in which participants must select an option.

Second, training should entail an exploration, discussion, deliberation, analysis and insight into relevant issues and not merely an enumeration of facts, figures and details. Indeed, all procedures, sequences and other lists of information should be readily accessible to employees in their work environment. They should not have to memorise inventories of information. They should be permitted to utilise textbooks and other references during examinations. When participants need to memorise details during training sessions or examinations, they tend to learn by rote. They memorise the facts without fully comprehending the material; they do not apply the material or adapt it to fulfil their needs.

To ensure that participants do not merely endeavour to out-perform one or two colleagues, managers and instructors must not introduce programs in which only a limited proportion of employees will fail some task. For example, they should not institute a training program in which only 10% of employees do not pass successfully. Instead, if necessary, incentives should be bestowed upon the 10% of employees who perform most successfully. These employees, for instance, could be encouraged to impart this material to other individuals in the future.

Staff Turnover

Regardless of the provisions that employees can access, or the training they can receive, individuals will inevitably leave the organisation. These departures often aggravate the pressures and difficulties that pervade the workplace. Several consultancies in Australia offer services that are intended to boost the retention of company staff but their effectiveness may not always be obvious. Fifteen of the twenty employees in one of these consultancies departed from the own organisation within a 6-month period.

Indeed, although inadvertent, recruiters and managers often select job applicants who are likely to depart prematurely. For example, when organisations seek salespersons, they tend to reject applicants who portray themselves as impatient, restless and impulsive. Yet some recent research contends that such applicants are actually more likely to remain at the organisation. They are actually more devoted and loyal to the company in which they are employed (Parks & Waldo, 1999).

In particular, salespersons who are not impatient, restless or impulsive prefer to work systematically and methodically. They prefer to plan tasks carefully and precisely, yet the sales role demands considerable flexibility. These plans, therefore, often need to be modified, amended or even disregarded altogether. Salespersons who formulate precise plans and specific goals experience frustration, resentment and disappointment. Their loyalty declines and their commitment diminishes.

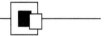

> *Instructors should ensure the structure of their training programs is not specified in its entirety. The participants themselves should attempt to identify topic headings, ascertain how each section aligns with the overall theme and consider the practical implications of the knowledge they acquire.*

Some managers, however, conceal the prospect that employees might want to leave. They pretend that everyone *should* remain loyal and should stay; they feel ashamed if individuals leave. Research indicates this shame is unnecessary. Most managers do not recognise the rate of turnover is unrelated to workplace performance. In the consummate workplace, ineffective employees leave more often that do effective employees. In many mismanaged workplaces, effective employees are more likely to leave than are ineffective employees. But, in both instances, turnover provides an opportunity to import a fresh outlook and a fresh approach (Beadles II, Lowery, Petty, & Ezell, 2000).

Therefore, in organisations in which effective employees are more likely to leave than ineffective employees, the incentive scheme might need to be scrutinised, adjusted or even overhauled. Specifically, remuneration should become more contingent upon the performance of employees. Employees who realise their goals, facilitate their colleagues and demonstrate ethical behaviour should receive more extensive bonuses. They should assume more responsibility and should experience more satisfaction. Bonuses should be increased gradually and wages should be maintained temporarily. Effective employees should remain and ineffective employees will depart.

Second, when an employee leaves the organisation, managers dread that a spate of departures will follow. They fear that all the friends and colleagues of this employee will also leave. But, this chain reaction seldom ensues. A few employees might feel inspired to leave or might feel a sudden burst of inspiration or a need to expand their horizons and develop their skills. But, according to recent scientific findings, these employees will not leave if the organisation offers a diverse range of training opportunities or if the organisation convenes many social functions (Krausz, Yaakobovitz, Bizman, & Caspi, 1999).

The colleagues of individuals who leave should be present at most exit interviews, whenever possible.

Nevertheless, before employees leave the organisation, a meeting should be convened between themselves, their peers and their managers. The motivations of these employees to leave — such as pay or workload — should be discussed openly and candidly. Their colleagues will thus feel that managers might adapt the workplace in the future to resolve these issues. They feel that managers will address the current problems that impede job satisfaction and that the workplace will be more inviting and more suitable to their needs.

Chapter 7

Recruitment and Selection

Recruitment

Even when the best initiatives are introduced to optimise retention, employees will occasionally leave and managers will need to source and select appropriate replacements. In larger organisations, managers may seek the services of a recruitment firm, a consultant or a specialist in human resources. Nevertheless, the managers will usually be involved in this process themselves and be granted the prerogative of reaching the final decision.

Any manager can attract applicants effectively — but few managers can attract effective applicants. For example, some managers will distribute advertisements that portray the work environment as friendly, supportive and understanding. Scholars have recently determined the unrecognised limitations of these campaigns (see Trank, Rynes, & Bretz Jr., 2002). Admittedly, these advertisements will attract many applicants who would like to work in such an environment, but they may not differentially attract suitable candidates. They may not specifically entice competent, gifted, insightful and creative individuals.

In contrast, advertisements that portray the environment as challenging and demanding tend to attract suitable candidates. They tend to attract individuals who have many achievements and realised many goals. Such individuals have often experienced the excitement that follows the realisation of some challenging goal. These individuals enjoy challenging situations and blossom in difficult environments.

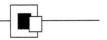

Job advertisements should emphasise the selection process as well as the position as being especially challenging and demanding.

To attract these candidates, job advertisements must first highlight the challenges the organisation offers. Such advertisements should emphasise the extensive training that is encouraged, the stringent criteria utilised during the selection process, the opportunities to receive promotions and the challenges and demands of the job.

Advertisements should emphasise the activities the organisation has undertaken to support the needs of employees, minorities, community groups or the wider environment. Perhaps the organisation has instituted a unique, ingenious program to support the needs of disabled employees or perhaps it offers jobs to homeless children. Apart from the support and relief these programs confer to so many deprived individuals, such causes also tend to attract suitable, gifted and effective candidates (Albinger & Freeman, 2000). Only such applicants can afford to reject offers from organisations that do not support individuals and communities. Thus, advertisements that emphasise these programs have been demonstrated to differentially attract suitable, desirable candidates.

Job Interviews

Unfortunately, some managers can attract, but not retain, job candidates. Many managers and recruiters, for example, aggravate the anxiety of these applicants. Either deliberately or unconsciously, managers and recruiters might want to induce some anxiety, perhaps to ascertain how the candidate responds to this strain. They might challenge, criticise or doubt applicants to assess their behaviour.

However, candidates who respond unsuitably might not actually be unsuitable at all. Candidates who respond inappropriately might simply doubt the applicability of this job or organisation or might decide the job and organisation does not fulfil their needs or desires.

Conversely, to address the doubts of candidates, some managers will inflate the benefits and trivialise the drawbacks of the organisation. They will highlight the camaraderie, innovations, progress and support but neglect aspects such as the management deficiencies, the extravagant workload or the tight surveillance. As expected, these candidates become more likely to accept the offers they receive and to perceive this organisation as suitable. However studies reveal that these candidates are more likely to leave the organisation within a few months (e.g., Buckley et al., 2002) and are more likely to squander the recruitment, induction and training costs that have been invested to develop their skills.

Recruiters and managers should thus follow a series of recommendations that accommodate these issues. They should first reduce applicants' unease during job interviews and display appreciation and empathy towards this anxiety and tension. They should encourage the applicant to express their feelings; perhaps by describing instances in which they experienced similar emotions, concerns and doubts. They may specify some of the questions they will ask candidates in advance, primarily to alleviate this anxiety.

Second, managers should specify some of the potential drawbacks of the job. They should be frank with candidates and honest to the individuals who could advance the organisation. They should then justify their decision to emphasise these drawbacks, particularly mentioning that job candidates often leave organisations prematurely because they are oblivious to these factors. Many candidates are not primed to accommodate, accept, address or resolve these drawbacks. Indeed, managers should perhaps describe an instance in which they were disappointed with a job in another organisation. This information can help candidates to become less likely to forge unrealistic expectations, less likely to leave prematurely and thus less likely to squander resources.

Personnel Selection

The difficult facet of recruitment is seldom *how* to retain but rather *who* to retain. Many common techniques used to identify suitable candidates are in fact flawed, misleading or futile. For example, a recruiter will often ask candidates to specify how they would respond to a hypothetical incident: perhaps an insolent employee, an unrealistic deadline or a demanding customer. Unfortunately, research reveals that candidates who respond suitably — those who describe an action the recruiter believes is appropriate — are no more likely to enhance workplace performance than are other candidates (see Taylor & Small, 2002). Candidates might know how to act appropriately — but they may lack the motivation, desire or ability to act appropriately.

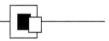

During job interviews, recruiters should concede some of the difficulties that pervade the organisation as well as the strengths. In particular, recruiters should focus on difficulties and instances in which they experienced anxiety. When recruiters concede their own anxiety, they appear more empathic and understanding, which can alleviate the distress that job applicants experience.

A recruiter might instead ask candidates to specify how they responded to previous incidents. How did they reach some decision, confront some colleague, overcome some weakness or respond to some criticism? Candidates who respond appropriately to these questions — according to the recruiter — have been shown to receive more favourable evaluations from their supervisor a year later (see Taylor & Small, 2002). This finding has been touted as evidence that responses to past incidents can be used to identify suitable candidates — to demonstrate that previous behaviour predicts future performance.

Occasionally, this finding is confirmed but usually, this assumption is misleading, as revealed by Huffcutt and colleagues in 2001. Candidates who respond appropriately to these questions might be perceived as effective by supervisors, but do not enhance workplace performance any more than other applicants nor do they promote innovation or cooperation more than other individuals.

Instead, these candidates merely tend to be more sociable, assertive and manipulative. They are more likely to highlight, inflate and exaggerate their merits, achievements and deeds to impress both their recruiters and supervisors. They are more likely to be *perceived* as effective. They are not, however, more likely to be effective and indeed, they are usually less likely to acquire skills, assist colleagues, propose initiatives and advance the workplace.

Likewise sociable, assertive, manipulative candidates tend to be perceived as more skilled or more qualified. They tend to embellish their skills and experiences. Candidates who are not especially sociable or authoritative do not underscore their qualifications. Thus, even if more experienced and qualified, they are perceived as less skilled and knowledgeable than sociable, assertive and manipulative applicants (Kristof-Brown, Barrick, & Franke, 2002). To override this bias, the skills, knowledge and qualifications of candidates should be derived from a survey, not an interview. Interviews should be used sparingly. They should be used to extract information that cannot be determined through other means.

The importance of sociability in job applicants was highlighted by Ferris, Witt and Hochwarter in 2001 in a study involving a survey of a large cohort of engineers. This survey determined the extent to which these engineers were sociable, as well as their level of intelligence and salary. Engineers whose intelligence was limited were more likely to receive a high salary if they were perceived as reserved and unsociable, rather than gregarious and extraverted. That is, employees who are sociable are less likely to devote effort into skill development. Instead, they dedicate their efforts to the formation of relationships, which might not promote their performance. In addition, managers often have higher expectations of achievement with sociable employees and thus might be more disillusioned with the performance of these gregarious individuals.

Similarly, almost no other characteristics or attributes always enhance behaviour. For example, methodical and disciplined candidates are usually regarded as suitable; indeed these systematic, careful and responsible applicants reflect the consummate employee. Scientists, however, have identified some unexpected deficits in these individuals (Witt, Brown, Barrick, & Mount, 2002). Specifically, even these individuals are usually too rigid, too inflexible or too conventional — especially if they also tend to be assertive and independent. As a consequence, most personality inventories are futile. While they delineate the personality profile of applicants, they do not present the repercussions of these attributes or unearth the implications of these traits.

Furthermore, many recruiters and managers rely on popular, fashionable measures to select applicable candidates. For example, many recruiters now measure the emotional intelligence of applicants. These measures assess the extent to which candidates can recognise, appreciate, describe, leverage, manipulate and regulate emotions in themselves and other individuals. Applicants who exhibit emotional intelligence are preferred, indeed desired; applicants who exhibit limited emotional intelligence are slighted and disdained.

Recent studies have challenged this practice to some extent (Elfenbein & Ambady, 2002). Employees who demonstrate emotional intelligence are sometimes ineffective, inappropriate and inferior. For instance, these employees can often readily decipher unpleasant emotions from the voice of their colleagues. They can detect when a colleague is anxious or irritated, even when this individual pretends to feel confident or composed. These employees are thus aware of the anxiety, gloom and irritation in other colleagues and therefore, they are less likely to trust colleagues. They are less likely to respond as their colleague had hoped and anticipated and less likely to be valued by these individuals.

Managers should select applicants who strive to improve their own skills and assign shortfalls to their own errors as they are more likely to demonstrate insight and creativity (Janssen & Van Yperen, 2004). These candidates are more likely to exhibit resilience to stress and to demonstrate receptivity to criticism. They are more likely to experience passion and motivation during training programs or to demonstrate few, if any, salient faults.

Job interviews should be utilised to select applicants who strive to improve their own skills and assign shortfalls to their own errors. Personality tests that can uncover deficiencies or traits that applicants attempt to conceal should also be considered.

During job interviews, managers can also ascertain the candidates' values and priorities. Managers should specifically assess the value that candidates attach to significant factors, such as: cooperation versus personal achievement, family versus work, variety versus stability, or hierarchy versus equality. To assess these priorities, managers must portray each alternative in the various pairs as equally desirable. Candidates whose values coincide with the responses of colleagues should be selected preferentially (Hegtvedt, Clay-Warner, & Ferrigno, 2002).

Despite this abundance of research, many managers may rely on their own intuition or instinct rather than analysis, validated instruments, or formal processes. Managers who apply this approach have been shown to select unsuitable candidates. Furthermore, managers who select candidates or strategic allies to whom they have formed a bond or relationship tend to undermine workplace performance (Saxton, 1997).

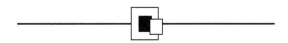

Chapter 8

Conclusions

Having read this far, some readers may still remain unconvinced that the science of management should replace many current beliefs about how to manage people. Perhaps you feel that disparities between common beliefs and scientific discoveries do not necessarily represent misconceptions. The scientists themselves might be mistaken or they might not have unearthed the bona fide truth.

Managers and supervisors often feel that academics are too academic and scientists are too scientific. That is, they feel that scientists disregard the intricacies that pervade every workplace and the complexities that complicate every decision. These intricacies and complexities can be appreciated only through experience, not science.

This criticism, however, does not apply to any of the scientific discoveries that are presented in this book. In most instances, these scientific discoveries evolved from the insights and experiences of a diverse range of managers and employees. Over time, these insights were then collated and distilled to form theories and propositions. These theories and propositions have been subjected to an extensive range of scientific procedures to evaluate their legitimacy.

Second, some enlightened readers are aware that many prevalent, but preventable, shortcomings compromise the utility and validity of numerous scientific studies. Scientists themselves have uncovered a host of technical shortfalls that plague many research programs — shortfalls with pretentious names such as untenable statistical assumptions, deficient statistical power, confounded treatments, asymmetric transfer, spurious relationships or ambiguous causal direction.

For example, in the past, many researchers have been commissioned to unearth the hallmarks of excellent companies. In some of these studies, however, the characteristics of unsuccessful companies were not explored. As a consequence, the characteristics of successful companies — such as assertive CEOs or comprehensive market analyses — may be equally ubiquitous in unsuccessful companies. Without a legitimate comparison group, the findings of these studies are entirely futile.

Fortunately these shortfalls do not challenge the scientific discoveries this book presents. Instead, this book presented only the discoveries in which these limitations have been circumvented or minimised. To satisfy managers with a penchant for science, we can specify some of the criteria that were applied to discard unsuitable findings. For example, conservative levels of *alpha* were utilised to accommodate violations of statistical assumptions, non-significant effects were omitted to circumvent instances of deficient power, and findings that do not align with a solid theory were excluded.

This does not mean that such scientific insights are always accurate. Scientific theories are not incontrovertible statements, impervious to doubt or reproach. Instead, scientific discoveries — insights from the congruence of many opinions and the findings of many systematic examinations — are more likely to be useful and unbiased than will the intuitive beliefs of managers and employees.

This book has presented a wide range of scientific discoveries that differ from most managers' and employees' beliefs and practices. These misconceptions impair managers' capacity to fulfil their role effectively. Their employees are less likely to feel inspired, driven, composed, satisfied or committed. When managers operate on invalid assumptions, they are less likely to perform efficiently, to demonstrate initiative, to cooperate effectively, to operate safely, to satisfy customers or to tolerate diversity. Such managers seldom earn respect, communicate proficiently, evaluate other individuals accurately and, most importantly, they seldom redress their limitations and shortcomings.

After reading this far, you may feel uneasy that many of your beliefs, opinions, instincts and behaviours are no longer indisputable. They are no longer beyond reproach. Your confidence might diminish or your inspiration might decline.

This despair, however, is unfounded. This book focuses solely on the misconceptions that are rife in our society or prevalent in management and intentionally overlooks a multitude of beliefs and opinions that align with scientific findings. Hence this book may have obscured the inspiring realisation that our beliefs and behaviours are usually appropriate; they are usually compatible with the ideals that scientists espouse.

Intuition and instincts are never to be disregarded. You should not supplant your intuition and instincts with the rules and principles of this or any other book. Indeed, scientific studies themselves underscore the importance of intuition and instinct. These studies reveal that some individuals reach decisions impulsively and effortlessly rather than carefully and systematically and are more likely to reach suitable decisions than are other employees.

Compared to their cautious, methodical counterparts, these individuals tend to reach more appropriate decisions whenever the issue involves many uncertain, conflicting considerations — the hallmark of most important judgments (see McMackin & Slovic, 2000; Riding & Wigley, 1997). Only intuition and instinct can accommodate the mass of complications that need to be considered.

Thus, clearly you should develop, rather than disregard, intuition — that reservoir of implicit knowledge, skills and assumptions that can guide your decisions and enhance your behaviour. At regular intervals, you might consider following one of the suggestions or sharing with a colleague one of the insights this book offers. Over time, these practices will redress the misconceptions that impair performance and will refine intuition and ensure that instincts optimise behaviour.

The authors sincerely hope that readers will have found this work helpful. Should there be any suggestions for improvement, or other interesting ideas, they would be delighted to hear from you.

Melbourne
February 2005
simon.moss@med.monash.edu.au
ronald.francis@med.monash.edu.au

References

This extensive reference list is included to enable readers with an appropriately sceptical disposition to assess for themselves the claims this book presents.

Albinger, H.S., & Freeman, S.J. (2000). Corporate social performance and attractiveness as an employer to different job seeking populations. *Journal of Business Ethics, 28*, 243–253.

Allan, S., & Gilbert, P. (2002). Anger and anger expression in relation to perceptions of social rank, entrapment and depressive symptoms. *Personality and Individual Differences, 32*, 551–565.

Antonioni, D., & Park, H. (2001). The relationship between rater affect and three sources of 360-degree feedback ratings. *Journal of Management, 27*, 479–495.

Apter, M.J., Mallows, R., & Williams, S. (1998). The development of the motivational style profile. *Personality and Individual Differences, 24*, 7–18.

Aquino, K. (1998). The effects of ethical climate and the availability of alternatives on the use of deception during negotiation. *International Journal of Conflict Management, 9*, 195–217.

Ariely, D., & Wertenbroch, K. (2002). Procrastination, deadlines, and performance: Self-control by precommitment. *Psychological Science, 13*, 219–224.

Aschoff, J.A. (1998). Human perception of short and long time intervals: Its correlation with body temperature and the duration of wake time. *Journal of Biological Rhythms, 13*, 437–442.

Ayers, D., Dahlstrom, R., & Skinner, S.J. (1997). An exploratory investigation of organizational antecedents to new product success. *Journal of Marketing Research, 34*, 107–116.

Bachrach, D.G., Bendoly, E., & Podsakoff, P.M. (2001). Attributions of the "causes" of group performance as an alternative explanation of the relationship between organizationl citizenship behavior and organizational performance. *Journal of Applied Psychology, 86*, 1285–1293.

Bacon, N., & Blyton, P. (2002). Militant and moderate trade union orientations: What are the effects of workplace trade unionism, union-management relations and employee gains? *International Journal of Human Resource Management, 13*, 302–319.

Banfield, J.F., Pendry, L.F., Mewse, A.J., & Edwards, M.G. (2003). The effects of an elderly stereotype prime on reaching and grasping actions. *Social Cognition, 21,* 299–319.

Bargh, J.A., Gollwitzer, P.M., Lee-Chai, A., Barndollar, K., & Trotschel, R. (2001). The automated will: Nonconscious activation and pursuit of behavioral goals. *Journal of Personality and Social Psychology, 81,* 1014–1027.

Beadles II, N.A., Lowery, C.M., Petty, M.M., & Ezell, H. (2000). An examination of the relationships between turnover functionality, turnover frequency, and organizational performance. *Journal of Business and Psychology, 15,* 331–337.

Beal, D.J., Ruscher, J.B., & Schnake, S.B. (2001). No benefit of the doubt: Intergroup bias in understanding causal explanation. *British Journal of Social Psychology, 40,* 531–543.

Begley, T.M., Lee, C., & Czajka, J.M. (2000). The relationships of type A behavior and optimism with job performance and blood pressure. *Journal of Business and Psychology, 15,* 215–227.

Ben-Ari, O.T., Florian, V., & Mikulincer, M. (2000). Does a threat appeal moderate reckless driving. A terror management theory perspective. *Accident Analysis and Prevention, 32,* 1–10.

Bersen, Y., Shamir, B., Avolio, B.J., & Popper, M. (2001). The relationship between vision strength, leadership style, and context. *Leadership Quarterly, 12,* 53–73.

Bizman, A., & Yinon, Y. (2001). Intergroup and interpersonal threats as determinants of prejudice: The moderating role of ingroup identification. *Basic and Applied Social Psychology, 23,* 191–196.

Blair, R.J.R. et al. (2002). Turning a deaf ear to fear: Impaired recognition of vocal affect in psychopathic individuals. *Journal of Abnormal Psychology, 111,* 682–686.

Blantan, H., Axsom, D., McClive, K.P., & Price, S. (2001). Pessimistic bias in comparative evaluations: A case of perceived vulnerability to the effects of negative life events. *Personality and Social Psychology Bulletin, 27,* 1627–1636.

Bono, J.E., Boles, T.L., Judge, T.A., & Lauver, K.J. (2002). The role of personality in task and relationship conflict. *Journal of Personality, 70,* 311–344.

Boone, C., De Brabander, B., Carree, M., de Jong, G., van Olffen, W., & van Witteloostuijin, A. (2002). Locus of control and learning to cooperate in a prisoner's dilemma game. *Personality and Individual Differences, 32,* 929–946.

Bragger, J.D. (2003). When success breeds failure: History, hysteresis, and delayed exit decisions. *Journal of Applied Psychology, 88.* 6–14.

Brennan, A., Chugh, J.S., & Kline, T. (2002). Traditional versus open offie design: A longitudinal field study. *Environment and Behavior, 34,* 279–299.

Brown, J.D., Farnham, S.D., & Cook, K.E. (2002). Emotional responses to changing feedback: Is it better to have won and lost than never to have won at all. *Journal of Personality, 70,* 127–141.

Brown, J.D., Farnham, S.D., & Cook, K.E. (2002). Emotional responses to changing feedback: Is it better to have won and lost than never to have won at all. *Journal of Personality, 70,* 127–141.

Brown, K.A., Willis, P.G., & Prussia, G.E. (2000). Predicting safe employee behavior in the steel industry: Development and test of a sociotechnical model. *Journal of Operations Management, 18,* 445–465.

Buckley, M.R., Mobbs, T.A., Mendoza, J.L., Novicevic, M.M., Carraher, S.M., & Beu, D.S. (2002). Implementing realistic job previews and expectation-lowering procedures: A field experiment. *Journal of Vocational Behavior, 61*, 263–278.

Buller, D.B., Borland, R., & Burgoon, M. (1998). Impact of behavioural intention on effectiveness of message features: Evidence from the family sun safety project. *Human Communication Research, 24*, 433–453.

Bushman, B.J., Baumeister, R.F., & Phillips, C.M. (2001). Do people aggress to improve their mood? Catharsis beliefs, affect regulation opportunity, and aggressive responding. *Journal of Personality and Social Psychology, 81*, 17–32.

Cannon-Bowers, J.A., Salas, E., Blickensderfer, E., & Bowers, C.A. (1998). The impact of cross-training and workload on team functioning: A replication and extension of initial findings. *Human Factors, 40*, 92–99.

Chan, E., & Ybarra, O. (2002). Interaction goals and social information processing: Underestimating one's partners but overestimating one's opponents. *Social Cognition, 20*, 409–439.

Chatman, J.A., & Flynn, F.J. (2001). The influence of demographic heterogeneity on the emergence and consequences of cooperative norms in work teams. *Academy of Management Journal, 44*, 956–974.

Choi, I., & Nisbett, R.E. (1998). Situational salience and cultural differences in the correspondence bias and actor-observer bias. *Personality and Social Psychology Bulletin, 24*, 949–960.

Ciarocco, N.J., Summer, K.J., & Baumeister, R.F. (2001). Ostracism and ego depletion: The strains of silence. *Personality and Social Psychology Bulletin, 27*, 1156–1163.

Clapham, M.M. (2001). The effects of affect manipulation and information exposure on divergent thinking. *Creativity Research Journal, 13*, 335–350.

Conlon, D.E., & Hunt, C.S. (2002). Dealing with feeling: The influence of outcome representations on negotiation. *International Journal of Conflict Management, 13*, 38–58.

Cooke, R., & Sheeran, P. (2004). Moderation of cognition-intention and cognition-behaviour relations: A meta-analysis of properties of variables from the theory of planned behaviour. *British Journal of Social Psychology, 43*, 159–186.

Cooper, M.L., Agocha, V.B., & Sheldon, M.S. (2000). A motivational perspective on risky behaviors: The role of personality and affect regulatory processes. *Journal of Personality, 68*, 1059–1088.

Coughlan, R., & Connolly, T. (2001). Predicting affective responses to unexpected outcomes. *Organizational Behavior and Human Decision Processes, 85*, 211–225.

Coulson, M. (2004). Attributing emotion to static body postures: Recognition accuracy, confusions, and viewpoint dependence. *Journal of Nonverbal Behavior, 28*, 117–139

Cury, F., Elliot, A., Sarrazin, P., Fonseca, D.D,, & Rufo, M. (2002). The trichotomous achievement goal model and intrinsic motivation: A sequential mediational analysis. *Journal of Experimental Social Psychology, 38*, 473–481.

Davies, M.F. (1997). Evaluation of self-relevant information: Acceptance of favourable and unfavourable personality statements as feedback vs test items. *Personality and Individual Differences, 23*, 869–875.

DeChurch, L.A., & Marks, M.A. (2001). Maximizing the benefits of task conflict: The role of conflict management. *International Journal of Conflict Management, 12*, 4–22.

Desmond, P.A., & Matthews, G. (1997). Implications of task-induced fatigue effects in-vehicle countermeasures to driver fatigue. *Accident Analysis and Prevention, 29*, 515–523.

Dijksterhuis, A. (2004). I like myself but I don't know why: Enhancing implicit self-esteem by subliminal evaluative conditioning. *Journal of Personality and Social Psychology, 86*, 345–355.

Domino, G., Short, J., Evans, A., & Romano, P. (2002). Creativity and ego defense mechanisms: Some exploratory empirical evidence. *Creativity Research Journal, 14*, 17–25.

Dorado, M.A., Medina, F.J., Munduate, L., Cisneros, I.F.J., & Euwema, M. (2002). Computer-mediated negotiation of an escalated conflict. *Small Group Research, 33*, 509–524.

Duffy, M.K., & Shaw, J.D. (2000). The Salieri Syndrome: Consequences of envy in groups. *Small Group Research, 31*, 3–23.

Elfenbein, H.A., & Ambady, N. (2002). Predicting workplace outcomes from the ability to eavesdrop on feelings. *Journal of Applied Psychology, 87*, 963–971.

Emmons, R.A., & McCullough, M.E. (2003). Counting blessings versus burdens: An experimental investigation of gratitude and subjective well-being in daily life. *Journal of Personality and Social Psychology, 84*, 377–389.

Endo, Y., Heine, S.J., & Lehman, D.R. (2000). Culture and positive illusions in close relationships: How my relationships are better than yours. *Personality and Social Psychology Bulletin, 26*, 1571–1586.

Ferris, G.R., Witt, L.A., & Hochwarter, W.A. (2001). Interaction of social skill and general mental ability on job performance and salary. *Journal of Applied Psychology, 86*, 1075–1082.

Finkelstein, L.M., Protolipac, D.S., & Kulas, J.T. (2000). The role of subordinate authoritarianism in cross-level extra-role relationships. *Journal of Psychology, 134*, 435–442.

Fitzsimons, G.M., & Kay, A.C. (2004). Languages and interpersonal cognition: Causal effects of variations in pronoun usage on perceptions of closeness. *Personality and Social Psychology Bulletin, 30*, 547–557.

Flanagin, A.J. (2000). Social pressures on organizational website adoption. *Human Communication Research, 26*, 618–646.

Fletcher, C., & Baldry, C. (2000). A study of individual differences and self-awareness in the context of multi-source feedback. *Journal of Occupational and Organizational Psychology, 73*, 303–319.

Folger, R., & Skarlicki, D.P. (1998). When tough times make tough bosses: Managerial distancing as a function of layoff blame. *Academy of Management Journal, 41*, 79–87.

Ford, C.M., & Gioia, D.A. (2000). Factors influencing creativity in the domain of managerial decision making. *Journal of Management, 26*, 705–732

Forgas, J.P. (1999). On feeling good and being rude: Affective influences on language use and request formulations. *Journal of Personality & Social Psychology, 76*, 928–939.

Forster, J., Friedman, R.S., & Liberman, N. (2004). Temporal construal effects on abstract and concrete thinking: Consequences for insight and creative cognition. *Journal of Personality and Social Psychology, 87*, 177–189.

Fox, C.R., & Weber, M. (2002). Ambiguity aversion, comparative ignorance, and decision context. *Organizational Behavior and Human Decision Processes, 88,* 476–498.

Fox, S., Spector, P.E., & Miles, D. (2001). Counterproductive work behavior (CWB) in response to job stressors and organizational justice: Some mediator and moderator tests for autonomy and emotions. *Journal of Vocational Behavior, 59,* 291–309.

Frank, M.G., & Ehkman, P. (2004). Appearing truthful generalizes across different deception situations. *Journal of Personality and Social Psychology, 86,* 486–495.

Fried, Y., Ben-David, H.A., Tiegs, R.B., Avital, N., & Yeverechyaha, U. (1998). The interactive effect of role conflict and role ambiguity on job performance. *Journal of Occupational and Organizational Psychology, 71,* 19–27.

Friedman, R.A., Tidd, S.T., Currall, S.C., & Tsai, J.C. (2000). What goes around comes around: The impact of personal conflict style on work conflict and stress. *International Journal of Conflict Management, 11,* 32–55.

Friedman, R.S., & Forster, J. (2002). The influence of approach and avoidance motor actions on creative cognition. *Journal of Experimental Social Psychology, 38,* 41–55.

Fritzsche, B.A., McIntire, S.A., & Yost, A.P. (2002). Holland type as a moderator of personality-performance predictions. *Journal of Vocational Behavior, 60,* 422–436.

Funderburg, S.A., & Levy, P.E. (1997). The influence of individual and contextual variables on 360-degree feedback system attitudes. *Group & Organization Management, 22,* 210–235.

Gardham, K., & Brown, R. (2001). Two forms of intergroup discrimination with positive and negative outcomes: Explaining the positive-negative asymmetry effect. *British Journal of Social Psychology, 40,* 23–34.

Geletkanycz, M.A., & Black, S.S. (2001). Bound by the past? Experience-based effects on commitment to the strategic status quo. *Journal of Management, 27,* 3–21.

Gellatly, I.R., & Luchak, A.A. (1998). Personal and organizational determinants of perceived absence norms. *Human Relations, 51,* 1085–1102.

George, J.M., & Zhou, J. (2001). When openness to experience and conscientiousness are related to creative behavior: An interactional approach. *Journal of Applied Psychology, 86,* 513–524.

Gonzales, M.H., Burgess, D.J., & Mobilo, L.J. (2001). The allure of bad plans: Implications of plan quality for progress towards possible selves and postplanning energization. *Basic and Applied Social Psychology, 23,* 87–108.

Grandey, A.A. (2003). When "The show must go on": Surface acting and deep acting as determinants of emotional exhaustion and peer-rated service delivery. *Academy of Management Journal, 46,* 86–96.

Green, J.D., & Sedikides, C. (2001). When do self-schemas shape social perception? The role of descriptive ambiguity. *Motivation and Emotion, 25,* 67–83.

Greenberg, L., & Barling, J. (1999). Predicting employee aggression against coworkers, subordinates, and supervisors: The roles of person behaviours and perceived workplace factors. *Journal of Organizational Behavior, 20,* 897–913.

Guimand, S., & Dambrum, M. (2002). When prosperity breeds intergroup hostility: The effects of relative deprivation and relative gratification on prejudice. *Personality and Social Psychology Bulletin, 28,* 900–912.

Gully, S.M., Payne, S.C., Koles, K.L.K., & Whiteman, J.K. (2002). The impact of error training and individual differences on training outcomes: An attribute-treatment interaction perspective. *Journal of Applied Psychology, 87,* 143–155.

Guthrie, J.P. (2000). Alternative pay practices and employee turnover. *Group & Organization Management, 25,* 419–439.

Haddock, G. (2002). It's easy to like or dislike Tony Blair: Accessibility experiences and the favourability of attitude judgments. *British Journal of Psychology, 93,* 257–267.

Harp, S.F., & Mayer, R.E, (1998). How seductive details do their damage: A theory of cognitive interest in science learning. *Journal of Educational Psychology, 90,* 414–434.

Haworth, C.L., & Levy, P.E. (2001). The importance of instrumentality beliefs in the prediction of organizational citizenship behaviors. *Journal of Vocational Behavior, 59,* 64–75.

Hegtvedt, K.A., Clay-Warner, J., & Ferrigno, E.D. (2002). Reactions to injustice: Factors affecting workers' resentment toward family-friendly policies. *Social Psychology Quarterly, 65,* 386–400.

Heilman, M.E., Wallen, A.S., Fuchs, D., & Tamkins, M.M. (2004). Penalties for success: Reactions to women who succeed at male gender-typed tasks. *Journal of Applied Psychology, 89,* 416–427.

Hill, R.W., McIntire, K., & Bacharach, V.B. (1997). Perfectionism and the Big Five factors. *Journal of Social Behavior and Personality, 12,* 257–270.

Ho, E.A., Sanbonmatsu, D.M., & Aikimoto, S.A. (2002). The effects of comparative status on social stereotypes: How the perceived success of some persons affects the stereotypes of others. *Social Cognition, 20,* 36–57.

Holmes, J.G., Miller, D.T., & Lerner, M.J. (2002). Committing altruism under the cloak of self-interest: The exchange fiction. *Journal of Experimental Social Psychology, 38,* 144–151.

Horowitz, L.M., et al. (2001). The way to console may depend on the goal: Experimental studies of social support. *Journal of Experimental Social Psychology, 38,* 49–61.

Houghton, S.M., Simon, M., Aquino, K., & Goldberg, C.B. (2000). No safety in numbers: Persistence of biases and their effects on team risk perception and team decision making. *Group & Organization Management, 25,* 325–353.

Howard, D.J. (1997). Familiar phrases as peripheral persuasion cues. *Journal of Experimental Social Psychology, 33,* 231–243.

Howard, D.J., & Gengler, C. (2001). Emotional contagion effects on product attitudes. *Journal of Consumer Research, 28,* 189–201.

Hsee, C.K., & Zhang, J. (2004). Distinction bias: Misprediction and mischoice due to joint evaluation. *Journal of Personality and Social Psychology, 86,* 680–695.

Huffcutt, A.I., Weekley, J.A., Wiesner, W.H., Degroot, T.G., & Jones, C. (2001). Comparison of situational and behavior description interview questions for higher-level positions. *Personnel Psychology, 54,* 619–644.

Hui, C., Lam, S.S.K., & Schaubroeck, J. (2001). Can good citizens lead the way in providing quality service? A field quasi experiment. *Academy of Management Journal, 44,* 988–995.

Hurley, A.E. (1997). The effects of self-esteem and source credibility on self-denying prophecies. *Journal of Psychology, 131,* 581–594.

REFERENCES

Igbaria, M., & Guimaraes, T. (1999). Exploring differences in employee turnover intentions and its determinants among telecommuters and non-telecommuters. *Journal of Management Information Systems, 16,* 147–164.

Iverson, R.D., & Erwin, P.J. (1997). Predicting occupational injury: The role of affectivity. *Journal of Occupational and Organizational Psychology, 70,* 113–128.

Jackson, L.M., Esses, V.M., & Burris, C.T. (2001). Contemporary sexism and discrimination: The importance of respect for men and women. *Personality and Social Psychology Bulletin, 27,* 48–61.

Janssen, O., & Van Yperen, N.W. (2004). Employees' goal orientations, the quality of leader-member exchange, and the outcomes of job performance and job satisfaction. *Academy of Management Journal, 47,* 368–384.

Jaussi, K.S., & Dionne, S.D. (2003). Leading for creativity: The role of unconventional leader behavior. *Leadership Quarterly, 14,* 475–498.

Jetten, J., Spears, R., & Manstead, A.S.R. (1997). Strength of identification and intergroup differentiation: The influence of group norms. *European Journal of Social Psychology, 27,* 603–609.

Kaiser, C.R., & Miller, C.T. (2001). Stop complaining: The social costs of making attributions to discrimination. *Personality and Social Psychology Bulletin, 27,* 254–263.

Kathuria, R. (2000). Competitive priorities and managerial performance: A taxonomy of small manufacturers. *Journal of Operations Management, 18,* 627–641.

Kawakami, K., Dovidio, J.F., & Dijksterhuis, A. (2003). Effect of social category priming on personal attitudes. *Psychological Science, 14,* 315–319.

Kay, A.C., & Jost, J.T. (2003). Complementary justice: Effects of "poor but happy" and "poor but honest" stereotype exemplars on system justification and implicit activation of the justice motive. *Journal of Applied Psychology, 85,* 823–837.

Keating, C.F., Randall, D.W., Kendrick, T., & Gutshall, K.A. (2003). Do babyfaced adults receive more help? The (cross-cultural) case of the lost resume. *Journal of Nonverbal Behavior, 27,* 89.

Kelly, A.E., Klusas, J.A., von Weiss, R.T., & Kenny, C. (2001). What is it about revealing secrets that is beneficial? *Personality and Social Psychology Bulletin, 27,* 651–665.

Kierein, N.M., & Gold, M.A. (2000). Pygmalian in work organizations: A meta-analysis. *Journal of Organizational Behavior, 21,* 913–928.

Koestner, R., Walker, M., & Fichman, L. (1999). Childhood parenting experiences and adult creativity. *Journal of Research in Personality, 33,* 92–107.

Korsgaard, M.A., Meglino, B.M., & Lester, S.W. (1997). Beyond helping: Do other-orientated values have broader implications in organizations. *Journal of Applied Psychology, 82,* 160–177.

Koslowsky, M., Sagie, A., Krausz, M., & Singer, A.D. (1997). Correlates of employee lateness: Some theoretical considerations. *Journal of Applied Psychology, 82,* 79–88.

Krausz, M., Yaakobovitz, N., Bizman, A., & Caspi, T. (1999). Evaluation of coworker turnover outcomes and its impact on the intention to leave of the remaining employees. *Journal of Business and Psychology, 14,* 95–107.

Kray, L.J., & Galinsky, A.D. (2003). The debiasing effect of counterfactual mind-sets: Increasing the search for disconfirmatory information in group decisions. *Organizational Behavior and Human Decision Processes, 91,* 69–81.

Kristof-Brown, A., Barrick, M.R., & Franke, M. (2002). Applicant impression management: Dispositional influences and consequences for recruiter perceptions of fit and similarity. *Journal of Management, 28*, 27–46.

Kuhl, J. (2000). A functional-design approach to motivation and volition: The dynamics of personality systems interactions. In M. Boekaerts, P. R. Pintrich, & M. Zeidner (Eds.), *Self-regulation: Directions and challenges for future research* (pp. 111–169). New York: Academic Press.

Lariscy, R. A. W., & Tinkhm, S. F. (1999). The sleeper effect and negative political advertising. *Journal of Advertising, 28*, 4-30.

Lassiter, G.D., & Munhall, P.J. (2001). The genius effects: Evidence for a nonmotivational interpretation. *Journal of Experimental Social Psychology, 37*, 349–355.

Lenton, S., Humeniuk, R., Heale, P., & Christie, P. (2000). Infringement versus conviction: The social impact of a minor cannabis offence in South Australia and Western Australia. *Drug and Alcohol Review, 19*, 257–264.

Levesque, C., & Pelletier, L.G. (2003). On the investigation of primed and chronic autonomous and heteronomous motivation orientation. *Personality and Social Psychology Bulletin, 29*, 1570–1584.

Levy, P.E., Cawley, B.D., & Foti, R.J. (1998). Reactions to appraisal discrepancies: Performance ratings and attributions. *Journal of Business and Psychology, 12*, 437–455.

Lewis, K.M. (2000). When leaders display emotion: How followers respond to negative emotional expression of male and female leaders. *Journal of Organizational Behavior, 21*, 221–234.

Linnenbrink, E.A., Ryan, A.M., & Pintrich, P.R. (2000). The role of goals and affect in working memory and functioning. *Learning and Individual Differences, 11*, 213–230.

Lopez, F.G. (2001). Adult attachment orientations, self-other boundary regulation, and splitting tendencies in a college sample. *Journal of Counselling Psychology, 48*, 440–446.

MacKenzie, S.B., Podsakoff, P.M., & Ahearne, M. (1998). Some possible antecedents and consequences of in-role and extra-role salesperson performance. *Journal of Marketing, 62*, 87–98.

Maio, G.R., & Olson, J.M, (1998). Attitude dissimulation and persuasion. *Journal of Experimental Social Psychology, 34*, 182–201.

Maio, G.R., Olson, J.M., Allen, L., & Bernard, M. (2001). Addressing discrepancies between values and behavior: The motivating effect of reasons. *Journal of Experimental Social Psychology, 37*, 104–117.

Malamut, A.B., & Offerman, L.R, (2001). Coping with sexual harassment: Personal, environmental, and cognitive determinants. *Journal of Applied Psychology, 86*, 1152–1166.

Martacchio, J.J., & Judge, T.A. (1997). Relationship between conscientiousness and learning in employee training: Mediating influences of self-deception and self-efficacy. *Journal of Applied Psychology, 82*, 764–773.

Martin, J.E., & Sinclair, R.R. (2001). A multiple motive perspective on strike propensities. *Journal of Organizational Behavior, 22*, 387–407.

Maxham J.G., III, & Netemeyer, R.G. (2002). A longitudinal study of complaining customers' evaluations of multiple service failures and recovery efforts. *Journal of Marketing, 66*, 57–71.

McCann, S.J.H. (2001). The precocity-longevity hypothesis: Earlier peaks in career achievement predict shorter lives. *Personality and Social Psychology Bulletin, 27,* 1429–1439.

McKendall, M., DeMarr, B., & Jones-Rikkers, C. (2002). Ethical compliance programs and corporate illegality: Testing the assumptions of the corporate sentencing guidelines. *Journal of Business Ethics, 37,* 367–383.

Meyer, J.P., Stanley, D.J., Herscovitch, L., & Topolnytsky, L. (2002). Affective, continuance, and normative commitment to the organization: A meta-analysis of antecedents, correlates, and consequences. *Journal of Vocational Behavior, 61,* 20–52.

Mikulay, S.M., & Goffin, R.D. (1998). Measuring and predicting counterproductivity in the laboratory using integrity and personality testing. *Educational and Psychological Measurement, 58,* 768–790.

Miller, D., & Lee, J. (2001). The people make the process: Commitment to employees, decision making, and performance. *Journal of Management, 27,* 163–189.

Miller, J.S., & Wiseman, R.M. (2001). Perceptions of executive pay: Does pay enhance a leader's aura. *Journal of Organizational Behavior, 22,* 703–711.

Mills, J., Cooper, D., & Forest, D. (2002). Polarization of interpersonal attraction: The effect of perceived potency. *Basic and Applied Social Psychology, 24,* 157–162.

Monin, B., & Miller, D.T. (2001). Moral credentials and the expression of prejudice. *Journal of Personality and Social Psychology, 81,* 33–43.

Montepare, J.M., & Dobish, H. (2003). The contribution of emotion perceptions and their overgeneralizations to trait impressions. *Journal of Nonverbal Behavior, 7,* 237–254.

Moore, S.C., & Oaksford, M. (2002). Some long-term effects of emotion on cognition. *British Journal of Psychology, 93,* 383–395.

Moorman, R.H., & Harland, L.K. (2002). Temporary employees as good citizens: Factors influencing their OCB performance. *Journal of Business and Psychology, 17,* 171–187.

Mumford, M.D. et al. (2002). Alternative approaches for measuring values: Direct and indirect assessments in performance prediction. *Journal of Vocational Behavior, 61,* 348–373.

Murphy, J.D., Driscoll, D.M., & Kelly, J.R. (2002). Differences in the nonverbal behavior or men who vary in the likelihood to sexually harass. *Journal of Social Behavior and Personality, 14,* 113–128.

Nauta, A., De Dreu, K.W., & Der Vaart, T.V. (2002). Social value orientation, organizational goal concerns and interdepartmental problem-solving behavior. *Journal of Organizational Behavior, 23,* 199–213.

Neuman, G.A., Wagner, S.H., & Christiansen, N.D. (1999). The relationship between work-team personality composition and the job performance of teams. *Group & Organization Management, 24,* 28–45.

Neumann, R. (2000). The causal influences of attributions on emotions: A procedural priming approach. *Psychological Science, 11,* 179–182.

North, A.C., Shimcock, A., & Hargreaves, D.J. (2003). The effect of musical style on restaurant customer's spending. *Environment and Behavior, 35,* 712–718.

O'Connor, B.P., & Dyce, J.A. (2001). Rigid and extreme: A geometric representation of personality disorders in five-factor model space. *Journal of Personality and Social Psychology, 81,* 1119–1130.

Okhuysen, G.A. (2001). Structuring change: Familiarity and formal interventions in problem-solving groups. *Academy of Management Journal, 44*, 794–808.

Oliver, R.L., & Anderson, E. (1994). An empirical test of the consequences of behavior- and outcome-based sales control systems. *Journal of Marketing, 58*, 53–67.

Oosterwegel, A., Field, N., Hart, D., & Anderson, K. (2001). The relation of self-esteem variability to emotion variability, mood, personality traits, and depression tendencies. *Journal of Personality, 69*, 689–708.

Paglis, L.L., & Green, S.G. (2002). Leadership self-efficacy and managers' motivation for leading change. *Journal of Organizational Behavior, 23*, 215–235.

Park, B., Wolsko, C., & Judd, C.M. (2001). Measurement of subtyping in stereotype change. *Journal of Experimental Social Psychology, 37*, 325–332.

Parker, S.K., & Axtell, C.M. (2001). Seeing another viewpoint: Antecedents and outcomes of employee perspective taking. *Academy of Management Journal, 44*, 1085–1100.

Parks, C.A., & Waldo, D. (1999). Assessing voluntary turnover likelihood using personality traits measured during pre-employment selection. *Current Research in Social Psychology, 4*, 135–145.

Phillippot, P., Schaefer, A., Herbette, G. (2003). Consequences of specific processing of emotional information: Impact of general versus specific autobiographical memory priming on emotion elicitation. *Emotion, 3*, 270–283.

Plaks, J.E., Stroessner, S.J., Dweck, C.S., & Sherman, J.W. (2001). Person theories and attention allocation: Preferences for stereotypic versus counterstereotypic information. *Journal of Personality and Social Psychology, 80*, 876–893.

Pluatania, J., & Moran, G.P. (2001). Social facilitation as a function of the mere presence of others. *Journal of Social Psychology, 141*, 190–197.

Powell, G.N., & Mainiero, L.A. (1999). Managerial decision making regarding alternative work arrangements. *Journal of Occupational and Organizational Psychology, 72*, 41–56.

Price, P.C., Pentecost, H.C., & Voth, R.D. (2002). Perceived event frequency and the optimistic bias: Evidence for a two-process model of personal risk judgments. *Journal of Experimental Social Psychology, 38*, 242–252. .

Rashotte, L.S. (2002). What does that smile mean? The meaning of nonverbal behaviours in social interaction. *Social Psychology Quarterly, 65*, 92–102.

Reiss, M.C., & Mitra, K. (1998). The effects of individual difference factors on the acceptability of ethical and unethical workplace behaviors. *Journal of Business Ethics, 17*, 1581–1593.

Reynolds, K.J., Turner, J.C., Haslam, A., & Ryan, M.K. (2001). The role of personality and group factors in explaining prejudice. *Journal of Experimental Social Psychology, 37*, 427–434.

Riding, R.J., & Wigley, S. (1997). The relationship between cognitive style and personality in further education students. *Personality and Individual Differences, 23*, 379–389.

Robbins, T.L., & DeNisi, A.S. (1998). Mood vs interpersonal affect: Identifying process and rating distortions in performance appraisal. *Journal of Business and Psychology, 12*, 313–325.

Rogelberg, S.G., Barnes-Farrell, J.L., & Creamer, V. (1999). Customer service behaviour: The interaction of service predisposition and job characteristics. *Journal of Business and Psychology, 13*, 421–435.

Rudawsky, D.J., Lungren, D.C., & Grasha, A.F. (1999). Competitive and collaborative responses to negative feedback. *International Journal of Conflict Management, 10,* 172–190.

Rudman, L.A., Greenwald, A.G., & McGhee, D.E. (2001). Implicit self-concept and evaluative implicit gender stereotypes: Self and ingroup share desirable traits. *Personality and Social Psychology Bulletin, 27,* 1164–1178.

Rudman, L.A., Greenwald, A.G., & McGhee, D.E. (2001). Implicit self-concept and evaluative implicit gender stereotypes: Self and ingroup share desirable traits. *Personality and Social Psychology Bulletin, 27,* 1164–1178.

Sarin, S., & Mahajan, V. (2001). The effect of reward structures on the performance of cross-functional product development teams. *Journal of Marketing, 65,* 35–53.

Saxton, T. (1997). The effects of partner and relationship characteristics on alliance outcomes. *Academy of Management Journal, 40,* 443–461.

Schneider, K.T., Swan, S., & Fitzgerald, L.F. (1997). Job-related and psychological effects of sexual harassment in the workplace: Empirical evidence from two organizations. *Journal of Applied Psychology, 82,* 401–415.

Scott, W.D., & Cervone, D. (2002). The impact of negative affect on personality standards: Evidence for an affect-as-information mechanism. *Cognitive Therapy and Research, 26,* 19–37.

Seibt, B., & Forster, J. (2004). Stereotype threat and performance: How self-stereotypes influence processing by inducing regulatory foci. *Journal of Personality and Social Psychology, 87,* 38–56.

Seta, J.J., Donaldson, S., & Seta, C.E. (1999). Self-relevance as a moderator of self-enhancement and self-verification. *Journal of Research in Personality, 33,* 442–462.

Settoon, R.P., & Adkins, C.L. (1997). Newcomer socialization: The role of supervisors, coworkers, friends and family members. *Journal of Business and Psychology, 11,* 507–516.

Shaw, J.C., Eric, W., & Colquitt, J.A. (2003). To justify or excuse? A meta-analytic review of the effects of explanations. *Journal of Applied Psychology, 88,* 444–458.

Shih, M., Ambady, N., Richeson, J.A., Fujita, K., & Gray, H.M. (2002). Stereotype performance boosts: The impact of self-relevance and the manner of stereotype activation. *Journal of Personality and Social Psychology, 83,* 638–647.

Shipper, F., & Davy, J. (2002). A model and investigation of managerial skills, employees' attitudes, and managerial performance. *Leadership Quarterly, 13,* 95–120.

Shore, T.H., Adams, J.S., & Tashchian, A. (1998). Effects of self-appraisal information, appraisal purpose, and feedback target on performance appraisal ratings. *Journal of Business and Psychology, 12,* 283–297.

Sigler, T.H., & Pearson, C.M. (2000). Creating an empowering culture: Examining the relationship between organizational culture and perceptions of empowerment. *Journal of Quality Management, 5,* 27–52.

Silvester, J., Anderson-Gough, F.M., Anderson, N.R., & Mohamed, A.R. (2002). Locus of control, attributions and impression management in the selection interview. *Journal of Occupational and Organizational Psychology, 75,* 59–76.

Singh, J. (1998). Striking a balance in boundary-spanning positions: An investigation of some unconventional influences of role stressors and job characteristics on job outcomes of salespeople. *Journal of Marketing, 62,* 69–86.

Slocombe, T.E., & Bluedorn, A.C. (1999). Organizational behavior implications of the congruence between preferred polychronicity and experienced work-unit polychronicity. *Journal of Organizational Behavior, 20,* 75–99.

Smyth, J.M. (1998). Written emotional expression: Effect sizes, outcome types, and moderating variables. *Journal of Consulting and Clinical Psychology, 66,* 174–184.

Soldat, A.S., Sinclair, R.C., & Mark, M.M. (1997). Color as an environmental processing cue: External affective cues can directly affect processing strategy without affecting mood. *Social Cognition, 15,* 55–71.

Sosik, J.L., & Megerian, L.E. (1999). Understanding leader emotional intelligence and performance. *Group & Organization Management, 24,* 367–390.

Stangor, C., Sechrist, G.B., & Jost, J.T. (2001). Changing racial beliefs by providing consensus information. *Personality and Social Psychology Bulletin, 27,* 486–496.

Stober, J. (1997). Trait anxiety and pessimistic appraisal of risk and chance. *Personality and Individual Differences, 22,* 465–476.

Strickland, O.J., & Galimba, M. (2001). Managing time: The effects of personal goal setting on resource allocation strategy and task performance. *Journal of Psychology, 135,* 357–367.

Swann, W.B., Jr., Kwan, V.S.Y., Polzer, J.T., & Milton, L.P. (2003). Fostering group identification and creativity in diverse groups: The role of individuation and self-verification. *Personality and Social Psychology Bulletin, 29,* 1396–1406.

Tang, T.L., & Ibrahim, A.H.S. (1998). Antecedents of organizational citizenship behavior revisited: Public personnel in the United States and in the Middle East. *Public Personnel Management, 27,* 529–550.

Taylor, P.J., & Small, B. (2002). Asking applicants what they would do versus what they did do: A meta-analytic comparison of situational and past behaviour employment interview questions. *Journal of Occupational and Organizational Psychology, 75,* 277–294.

Teidens, L.Z., & Linton, S. (2001). Judgment under emotional certainty and uncertainty: The effects of specific emotions on information processing. *Journal of Personality and Social Psychology, 81,* 973–988.

Thompson, C.A., Beauvais, L.L., & Lyness, K.S. (1999). When work-family benefits are not enough: The influence of work-family culture on benefit utilization, organizational attachment, and work-family conflict. *Journal of Vocational Behavior, 54,* 392–415.

Tiedens, L.Z., & Fragale, A.R. (2003). Power moves: Complementarity in dominant and submissive nonverbal behavior. *Journal of Personality and Social Psychology, 84,* 558–568.

Towler, A.J., & Dipboye, R.L. (2001). Effects of trainer expressiveness, organization, and trainee goal orientation on training outcomes. *Journal of Applied Psychology, 86,* 664–673.

Trank, C.Q., Rynes, S.L., & Bretz, R.D., Jr., (2002). Attracting applicants in the war for talent: Differences in work preferences among high achievers. *Journal of Business and Psychology, 16,* 331–345.

Tsuzuki, Y., & Matsui, T. (1998). Subordinates' J-P preferences as a moderator of their responses to supervisory structure behavior: A simulation. *Journal of Psychological Type, 45,* 21–28.

Turillo, C.J., Folger, R., Lavelle, J.J., Umphress, E.E., & Gee, J.O. (2002). Is virtue its own reward? Self-sacrificial decisions for the sake of fairness. *Organizational Behavior and Human Decision Processes, 89,* 839–865.

Twenge, J.M., Baumeister, R.F., Tice, D.M., & Stucke, T.S. (2000). If you can't join them, beat them: Effects of social exclusion on aggressive behaviour. *Journal of Personality and Social Psychology, 81,* 1058–1069.

Van Dyne, L., Jehn, K.A,, & Cummings, A. (2002). Differential effects of strain on two forms of work performance: Individual employee sales and creativity. *Journal of Organizational Behavior, 23,* 57–74.

Verplanken, B., & Holland, R.W. (2002). Motivated decision making: Effects of activation and self-centrality of values on choices and behavior. *Journal of Personality and Social Psychology, 82,* 434–447.

Vigoda, E. (2002). Stress-related aftermaths to workplace politics: The relationships among politics, job distress, and aggressive behavior in organizations. *Journal of Organizational Behavior, 23,* 571–591.

Walton, D., & McKeown, P.C. (2001). Drivers' biased perceptions of speed and safety campaign messages. *Accidents Analysis and Prevention, 33,* 629–640.

Wenzlaff, R.M., & Bates, D.E. (2000). The relative efficacy of concentration and suppression strategies of mental control. *Personality and Social Psychology Bulletin, 26,* 1200–1212.

Werner, C.M., Stoll, R., Birch, P., & White, P.H. (2002). Clinical validation and cognitive elaboration: Signs that encourage sustained recycling. *Basic and Applied Social Psychology, 24,* 185–203.

Wheeler, K.G. (2002). Cultural values in relation to equity sensitivity within and across cultures. *Journal of Managerial Psychology, 17,* 612–627.

White, G.L, & Taytroe, L. (2003). Personal problem-solving using dream incubation: Dreaming, relaxation, or waking cognition? *Dreaming, 13,* 193–209.

White, P.H., Sanbonmatsu, D.M., Croyle, R.T., & Smittipatana, S. (2002). Test of socially motivated underachievement: "Letting up" for others. *Journal of Experimental Social Psychology, 38,* 162–169.

Windschitl, P.D., Kruger, J., & Nus Simms, E. (2003). The influence of egocentricism and focalism on people's optimism in competitions: When what affects us equally affects me more. *Journal of Personality and Social Psychology, 85,* 389–408.

Witowski, T., & Streinsmeier-Pelster, J. (1998). Performance deficits following failure: Learned helplessness or self-esteem protection? *British Journal of Social Psychology, 37,* 59–71.

Witt, L.A., Brown, L.A., Barrick, M.R., & Mount, M.K. (2002). The interactive effects of conscientiousness and agreeableness on job performance. *Journal of Applied Psychology, 87,* 164–169.

Wittenbaum, G.M., Hubbell, A.P., & Zuckerman, C. (1999). Mutual enhancement: Toward an understanding of the collective preference for shared information. *Journal of Personality and Social Psychology, 77,* 967–978.

Wong, C., & Hui, C., & Law, K.S. (1998). A longitudinal study of the job perception-job satisfaction relationship: A test of the three alternative specifications. *Journal of Occupational and Organizational Psychology, 71,* 127–146.

Wong, C., & Law, K.S. (2002). The effects of leader and follower emotional intelligence on performance and attitude: An exploratory study. *Leadership Quarterly, 13,* 243–274.

Worchel, S. (1998). Social identity and individual productivity within groups. *British Journal of Social Psychology, 37,* 389–413.

Worchel, S., Jenner, S.M., & Hebl, M.R. (1998). Changing the guard: How origin of new leader and disposition of ex-leader affect group performance and perceptions. *Small Group Research, 29,* 436–451.

Yarmey, A.D. (2000). Retrospective duration estimations for variant and invariant events in field situations. *Applied Cognitive Psychology, 14,* 45–57.

Zhang, L. (2003). Does the big five predict learning approaches? *Personality and Individual Differences, 34,* 1431–1446.

Zimbardo, P.G., Keough, K.A., & Boyd, J.N. (1997). Present time perspective as a predictor of risky driving. *Personality and Individual Differences, 23,* 1007–1023.

INDEX

www.ingramcontent.com/pod-product-compliance
Ingram Content Group Australia Pty Ltd
76 Discovery Rd, Dandenong South VIC 3175, AU
AUHW011250130325
408272AU00010B/35

9 781875 378784